Ghostcircle: The Inside Story

By Hannah Barrick

© Hannah Barrick, 2018

The right of Hannah Barrick is to be identified as the
Author of the Work has been
asserted by her in accordance with the Copyright,
Design and Patents Act of 1988.

First Published in the United Kingdom in 2018
All rights reserved.
ISBN: 978-0-957415638

Ghostcircle Publishing

European address:
36a Elbe Street, Fulham, London, SW6 2QP

Web: www.ghostcircle.com

Cover and typesetting: by Karl Fallon

In loving memory of Florry Cleary

A wonderful grandmother and the strongest woman I know. I will never forget your unending encouragement and support.

Table of Contents

About the Author 6

Acknowledgements 8

Preface 11

Discovering Ghostcircle 14

Meet The Team – Hannah Barrick 24

Meet The Team – Karl Fallon 33

Meet The Team – Ben Clutton 40

Meet The Team – Patrick McNamara 46

Meet The Team – Tracy Edwards 53

Meet The Team – Jamie Wilkins 59

Greenways Farm 72

Binnenveld House 84

Schloss Erichsburg 98

Moosham Castle 113

Malaspina Castle 127

Suasmarez Manor 140

Clonony Castle 158

The Bell 166

England's Rose 186

Our Sixth Sense 204

Methods of Communication 208

Epilogue...212

About the Author

Hannah Barrick is a British Psychic-medium who started discovering her psychic gifts in her teens. She has a unique psychic connection to animals which she uses to help her in her work within the veterinary field, and also with her interest in writing. Having travelled through Europe with the paranormal group Ghostcircle, she decided to combine her interests in the paranormal with her passion for writing and document the experiences she has had in this book.

Hannah's writing talent has also led her to write articles for Phenomena Magazine, and CatWorld magazine, while also writing small pieces of poetry in her spare time. She is also interested in writing fiction, short stories and is working on her first novel. In her spare time, she has an interest in horse riding and travelling and hopes to extend her travels further in the future.

Acknowledgements

There have been many interesting people involved in the writing and creation of this book. I have been privileged enough to be surrounded by a lot of inspirational and supportive people, all of whom have played a vital part in the creation of this book and turned it from a mere idea into a reality.

Firstly, I would like to extend my gratitude to all the owners of the venues that featured in the Ghostcircle programmes, and to the many wonderful people we met in those properties who very generously allowed us access in order to film. It goes without saying that by working together we have had so many varied and fascinating interactions in each of these places. It has not just helped me write the stories in the pages that will follow, but also enriched our lives with the new experiences and the opportunities we have had for learning more about the paranormal world, and how it interacts with our own physical or material world.

First and foremost, I would also like to extend my thanks to Patrick McNamara and to Karl Fallon, because without you both, the inspiration for writing this book would not have been given to me and it has given me the opportunity to help, educate, and inspire people with an introduction to the wonders of the Spiritual world and the paranormal. I would also like to secondly thank Karl, as without your excellent camera work and director skills we would not have captured the unscripted stories in the Ghostcircle programmes. From that we would not have these wonderful experiences to view, and for me to write about. The support and encouragement from both of you has been priceless and I cannot thank you enough.

To Patrick McNamara; for all of the constant encouragement and teaching you have shared with us. Your steady encouragement has allowed us to grow and become confident in our own psychic abilities while we learn how to use and control them. You have also been helping us to understand each new paranormal experience we have had along the way. It has meant so much to have your wisdom and experience guiding us, and it has been a privilege to be part of Ghostcircle with you.

Of course not least, an enormous amount of gratitude goes to Jamie. Not only have you been by my side through all of the investigations we have done together, but your constant belief and faith in me has sustained me not only through the writing of this book, but throughout everything we have done along our discovery of the paranormal. It has been a journey we have taken together, and one I wouldn't change for the world.

My next thank you goes to Ben; for he brings the fun and laughter to our team. It has been amazing working with you, and I've enjoyed how you have brought your unique mediumistic abilities which added so much substance to our investigations. Your fun and laughter has also helped us to be a little more light-hearted when we have become too serious at times too!

Thank you to Tracy Edwards; for being a part of our team and allowing your own wonderful Mediumship to enrich the trips you have accompanied us on, and for not only adding to our investigations with your brilliant clairvoyance, but also allowing us to meet and be introduced to the wonderful Spirit guide Peter who works through you.

And finally, a special thank you to our backroom production team. That is, all of the Guides, Helpers and those in Spirit that have inspired us on this magical journey. You have been teaching us and allowing us to learn about and experience the Spirit world. Without your help, and there seems to be lots of help, the core of this book could not have been written.

Preface

It has been my privilege to accompany the Ghostcircle team on our many wonderful adventures and psychic investigations of haunted places throughout the UK, Ireland, and Europe. Our team has grown and we have seen many extraordinary forms of evidential phenomena to prove the existence of life after death. The evidence that we have captured will hopefully give many people comfort in the knowledge that their deceased loved ones are still living in another world, a spiritual world; and that they have not gone but have just started another part of their journey to which we will catch up with them, once ours is completed here.

My main intention with this book is not simply to recount the different phenomena we have captured (although certainly this could make a book in itself!), but to give my own personal view of our experiences. Many people will have seen the Ghostcircle series on television, or on our phone app, but I hope to give people a more in depth view on how we investigate each location, by recounting it through my own views and personal experiences.

Ghostcircle has been filming and investigating haunted locations for seven years now, and as well as capturing evidence of spirit, we have also learned more with each place we have visited of what works in an investigation, and what doesn't. We have also discovered new ways in which spirit can communicate to us that we were not aware of before!

Many people will view the 'end result' as it were of an investigation conducted by mediums, or an investigation carried out by a paranormal group. And perhaps this gives some inclination to think that it is conducted in a similar way and just as simple as conducting an interview, albeit with the interviewee being all but invisible to everyone barring the interviewer. In this volume, I hope to show that it is in fact more of a journey, as even a natural medium has to learn how to use the tools that he/she has been given in order to communicate effectively with spirit. The conditions have to be right, and above all, *there must be no fear!*

This leads me to another purpose of this book. My aim is to take away the fear surrounding the spirit world. Yes, there are dark aspects to the paranormal just as there are dark aspects to earthly life. However, more often than not it has been my experience that communication is given through benign or well-intentioned spirits or guides, and that most of the fear we experience is simply through a lack of knowledge on the situation a person is present in, and the anticipating of what may possibly occur (usually negatively) in that situation, and invariably it never does. So I invite you to read this book with an open mind, and I will share my experiences with you and take you on my own journey into the world of Ghostcircle. Welcome to the inside story!

Discovering Ghostcircle

When I was initially introduced to Ghostcircle, I already had a firm interest in the paranormal. I had always felt there was something bigger than ourselves and that there was more to life than what we could physically see, but no matter how hard I tried, I couldn't quite seem to put my finger on what it was.

Growing up, I would not say I was particularly religious or followed a particular faith, but I identified most with the teachings of Christianity and definitely believed in a God, or higher power. But some of the teachings of religion in general didn't sit comfortably with me. I am very inquisitive by nature, and I felt some aspects of religion seemed to raise more questions than answers. With religious teachings I always felt that I was not getting the complete picture in so many areas. It still felt as if there was something missing. So one afternoon, I sat on my own in a room. I had no idea who I was talking to, but I remember feeling as though there was something, or someone there with me listening intently, as if they knew what I was thinking and had been waiting for me to voice this. And so I said aloud; "If there is something more out there, something I can't see yet, I'm ready. I want to find out what it is." This proved to be the beginning of my discovery of the paranormal and the spiritual world. As the saying goes: *beware what you wish for!*

Soon after this I met Jamie Wilkins through a mutual friend. My friend knew of my interest in the paranormal, and mentioned that Jamie shared this interest too. I was intrigued so I contacted him and asked if he might share some of his experiences with me. Jamie told me of his interest in music, and I discovered that he had, at this time, already met Psychic Medium Patrick McNamara, that he had attended regular psychic circles and he had also started composing pieces of music for the Ghostcircle DVD's that they were currently producing. As we became closer friends, I loved hearing of his experiences of these physical circles, and so my interest in the whole subject grew from there.

Jamie and I started spending more time together, and gradually we became closer and started seeing each other romantically. By now he was writing music frequently, and he would also let me listen to some of the musical pieces he had composed for Ghostcircle, and I loved listening to the different intricate melodies that he created. His talent and composition in classical music was very clear to see, as each piece he wrote was and still is, unique each time.

After a while, Jamie introduced me to Patrick. I was fascinated with the incredibly accurate mediumistic ability he had, and felt encouraged at his down-to-earth approach to the subject. It became clear early on that he was extremely gifted and knowledgeable on the spiritual world and how it interacts with our own world.

Soon after this, I was kindly invited to take part in a physical circle. On the evening of the circle, I felt cautiously optimistic. I had no idea what to expect, but my curiosity was winning out over my uncertainty. As Patrick started building the energy, I realised I could feel a cold breeze around the bottom half of my legs. The temperature difference was unmistakeable as the breeze was *ice* cold. I looked around the room to see if any windows or doors were open, and saw they were not. Then Patrick explained that this was simply the energy building and getting stronger, but that it was nothing to be afraid of.

When he invited me to join him at a 'tent' (a small storage container used for spirit energy) he had set up, I nervously walked up. This tent consisted of a simple metal pole framework supporting a green and black cover. I knew from the start of the circle that nothing was concealed with in the 'tent' because I had watched the team set this up beforehand. Patrick explained to the group that this 'tent' was simply used as a focus for spirit to help build and store the energy that is used to create the phenomena we see. As I stood in front of the tent, Patrick asked me to place my hand in front of me. As I did so, I realised I could see what looked like faint blue lines coming from my fingers. At first, I thought it was a trick of the light. I looked away briefly and looked back, but no - it was still there. What's more is I could feel a resistance too, as if my hand was actually going through something or pushing against something in front of me.

I explained to Patrick what I was seeing, and he then explained that I was actually "putting my hand into a spirit" - this was why I could feel the slight resistance. I was quite shocked. I had truly seen nothing like this before. I had thought that the evening would be based on Patrick giving readings to people, or perhaps watching Patrick communicate with spirit, but we were actually seeing and feeling everything for ourselves, really experiencing the paranormal.

Not once were we told or suggested what we should, or should not be seeing, instead we were simply asked if we were experiencing anything, and if we were, to describe our experiences. This was the ultimate evidence for me, as I had experienced something tangible for myself and seen it with my own eyes - after all, you can't get anything better than first-hand evidence - and I was fascinated to learn more.

To my delight, I was invited a short while after to another circle and of course I jumped at the chance. This time I was less nervous as I knew more what to expect and how the evening would progress. I have to say, the highlight of all the Physical Mediumship experiments we do must be the flower movement. Patrick explained to us that the energy – the blue lines or 'rods' that we were actually seeing when we held our hands in front of us – they could be used by spirit to actually turn the flowers in our hands.

Even I have to admit that at first I didn't quite believe him. It just didn't seem possible that this could happen, it's not the movies. However, I was about to be proven wrong! After Patrick had built the energy in the circle, he asked us all to hold a flower firmly between our index finger and our thumb. We all did as instructed, and intrigued, I watched as Patrick moved his hand in a circular motion just above – but not touching – the flower. The circle sitter holding the flower described feeling as though it was almost 'pulling'. As I watched closely, I noticed I could see the petals of the flower moving. They looked as though they were folding back towards the centre of the flower, before folding back out again. Some petals looked as though they were shaking or waving.

At first I didn't say anything. I was thinking maybe I was seeing things, but then a couple of the other circle sitters gasped, exclaiming they could also see the petals moving and folding. As we continued to watch we then actually saw the flower start to turn! It is difficult to describe the feeling you have when you first witness this. In some ways, it almost feels surreal, as everything in our own limited experience tells us it cannot be happening, that it isn't possible. Yet here we were, witnessing this for ourselves, seeing it with our own eyes. There was no denying it. A second circle sitter then placed their hand on top of the fingers of the person holding the flower, so that it eliminated all possibility of them moving it themselves. However, the flower still moved and turned in their hand, much to the amazement of us all.

I hoped that I would have the privilege of attending more circles like this, and I was not disappointed. It was fascinating seeing for the first time, a glimpse of the life beyond. It quite literally felt like the veil between the two worlds had been pulled back, revealing the secrets that lay behind. A veil really had indeed been removed, although I had no idea at this point how much more I was to discover.

During this time period, I began to try and gather as much knowledge as I could on the paranormal. I bought books, watched videos, anything I could find – but undoubtedly the best source of learning (aside from experience), was from Patrick. Patrick McNamara had been a psychic medium for many years by this time, and if I am honest I have still yet to meet a medium with as extensive knowledge as his on all things paranormal.

As I began to learn more and more about Ghostcircle and physical mediumship, what I found most satisfying was the scientific angle that was applied in our experiments. It added far more substance to all the experiences we had, and it also enabled us to explain the phenomena to other circle sitters we met in the future. Rather than us simply saying 'this is happening but we don't know how or why', Patrick was able to explain in a very down-to-earth way, exactly what was causing certain phenomena, and also how the energy was being manipulated by spirit guides. What's even more interesting is; it can be repeated with different people in different environments and "still get the same results", just like a science experiment. This for me added even more credibility to the phenomena that we were experiencing. It was repeatable!!

It was around this time when I also began to notice my own abilities were growing outside of what we did in the circles. At first it was very subtle. I would sense people's emotions and thoughts much more strongly than I had previously, or that I would be able to pick up on the general atmosphere of a place we had visited. Then I began to occasionally see what looked like a hazy white halo around a person's head. I later understood that what I was actually seeing was the person's aura.

The first time this happened, I was with a group of friends. We were standing and I was listening to what they were saying, and suddenly I realised I could see a misty haze around them. It looked almost like a second outline of the person that had an ethereal light. I felt my heart jump into my mouth. I truly thought I was having double vision and that there was obviously something seriously wrong with my eyes or vision. I had a sudden sense of panic but over the coming weeks I soon learned that this was the beginning of being able to see a person's aura. I found that the more I accepted it, the stronger my ability with this grew, until I then started seeing flashes of colour within a person or animal's auric field. Acceptance really helped me deal with it.

I found it both thrilling and exciting. Although I was of course quite nervous at times, I never felt fearful. My curiosity and fascination of the new experiences I was having outweighed any uncertainty I felt. My mind and my abilities were expanding and opening, and it was an amazing experience. Before long I realised that I could also pick up on other people's thoughts. I would mention something in conversation, only for the other person to remark that they had just been thinking the same thing. This was my telepathic ability opening up.

Of course, most people I am sure can relate to this telepathic thinking at least one time in their life. There has probably been many a time when you have coincidentally mentioned something that a friend was also thinking about, and that is the point. Psychic ability isn't a mysterious unknown phenomenon. I don't believe in coincidences. Anybody can develop their sixth sense and many people likely use their psychic intuition to a certain extent without realising it.

As time went on I became more and more comfortable with my newfound abilities. My friendships within Ghostcircle grew and so did my own confidence. Ghostcircle as a team were becoming ever more ambitious and we then set our sights on filming not just for DVD's, but to also make a television series that would enable us to reach a wider audience and bring hope to many more people. When this was first discussed, it seemed like a total impossibility. None of us had any previous television experience, but we set our sights on our goal and collectively strove towards it as a team.

In the following chapters I will document some of the many interesting places we have travelled to, recounting our experiences of different countries we visited, talk about some of the people we met along the way, and some the sights we saw or the difficulties we faced in the locations we filmed at. Each place had its own unique story to tell. When we first set out I had no idea of the many colourful and interesting adventures that lay ahead. But, we packed the car up our gear and set off for our first filming trip, and so the journey with Ghostcircle began. In the next few chapters we can meet the current Ghostcircle team.

Meet The Team – Hannah Barrick

Q. How did you first realise you had a psychic gift?

I have always been able to 'sense' things that I realised other people could not see, but I suppose it only really dawned on me that I actually had a psychic gift very late on – actually when I first started filming with Ghostcircle. Our friend and medium Patrick McNamara described different psychic experiences and phenomenon and I soon realised that I also had a lot of these experiences over the years, not really knowing at the time what it was.

Q. How did you first realise you have an aptitude/talent for writing?

I have always enjoyed writing, and as child I would often write my own versions of my favourite children's books and make up my own stories. I also learned to read very quickly and impressed my teachers at school by being able to read advanced books from a young age. I first realised I had a real talent at writing though at the age of 14 when I entered a school poetry competition. Normally I dismissed entering any competitions, but for some reason I decided to enter this one just for the fun of it. I wrote a poem and sent it in. I didn't expect anything to come of it and completely forgot about the whole thing until I received a letter through the post saying that I had been one of the few entrants who had been selected to have their poem published in 'A Poetry Odyssey.' The volume aims at showcasing the work of young (school aged) poets. This encouraged me to continue writing, and I was also further encouraged years later after joining Ghostcircle, when the kind editor of Phenomena magazine agreed to publish an article I had written on my experiences filming with Ghostcircle.

Q. What work do you do outside of Ghostcircle?

Outside of Ghostcircle, I also have a strong interest in animals, and worked for four years in a veterinary surgery as a nursing assistant. Whilst working there I learned about veterinary nursing, animal health and husbandry, including caring for exotics such as rodents, birds (including birds of prey), and reptiles. I then worked for Blue Cross which is an Animal

Veterinary Charity. I found the experience very rewarding working for an organisation dedicated to helping owners unable to afford private fees for veterinary care of their pets. It is also rewarding being able to make a difference by answering people's questions and educating people on the general care of their pets.

Q. How did you develop an interest in animals?

It may sound strange, but growing up I always had a feeling of being 'different', and simply felt more comfortable in the company of animals. I noticed how animals respond and react differently to people – they respond to how they are treated rather than the judgements or first impressions they make of people. Having also an interest in science, I was fascinated with watching veterinary programs and enjoyed learning about animal biology and healthcare – this was later to become my motivation for starting to work in this field.

Q. When did you first realise you had a psychic connection with animals?

I discovered my psychic connection with animals whilst first working in a veterinary surgery by helping to nurse the sick or poorly animals. A lot of the time I would instinctively know what the animal needed, or even what they were feeling. On other occasions, I would sometimes notice a fuzzy light around them. I realized later on that this fuzzy light was their aura. Sometimes, If I had a little free time in the day, I would also spend a few minutes sending healing to the patients who most needed it – and more often than not the patients would respond, almost as if they were aware that they were receiving some help or healing. A lot of people simply call this a 'nurses instinct', and believe it is developed only simply because of their logical scientific training. However, from my experience I have realised that nine times out of ten it is actually the case that the nurse, on a psychic level, is picking up on the patient's need – often through the animal's aura. Anybody can develop this ability as it is intuitive, and not necessarily due to some form of formal training. Of course, in a veterinary setting, the nurses' training then allows them to act accordingly on this intuition. It is simply termed a 'nurses instinct' because people don't recognise what it truly is – their own psychic intuition.

Q. What do you enjoy most about travelling/filming with Ghostcircle?

This is a difficult one to answer. I would probably say that one of the things I enjoy most is the variety of beautiful and picturesque places that we visit. Each place has its own 'feeling' and atmosphere, and as mediums we are even more sensitive to these vibrations. It is also fascinating learning about the history of each individual place and seeing the architecture in a whole variety of countries. I really enjoy exploring and learning new things, and so it is amazing to see such a variety of places and people.

Q. Have you ever seen a spirit and can you describe the experience?

Well, there are lots of times where I have seen spirits, but the first time where I actually remember seeing a solid figure of a spirit was after I had started work. I was by this time working as a nursing assistant in a vet surgery, and one day as I was attending to one of the patients in the kennel room I very clearly saw someone a bit taller than me walk in through the door behind me and walk over to the sink in the corner of the room. I didn't see any features but the figure was solid enough that it blocked the light and I then felt a slight breeze as they walked past me. Thinking it was one of my colleagues in the room, without turning around I started talking about the patient I was attending and asking their opinion on what we should do. When I didn't receive a reply, I turned and saw that the room was empty and I was alone. When I asked all of my colleagues if they had been down there, all them said that they had not been into that room, although strangely one of the nurses told me later that it wasn't the first time that somebody had seen a ghost there, and that a number of my other colleagues had also had paranormal or strange experiences while working there.

Q. What other interests/hobbies do you have outside of Ghostcircle?

Outside of Ghostcircle I still enjoy writing short stories and poetry in my spare time. Some of my other interests include watching films, as well as horse riding - which I normally try to do at least once a week. More recently I have started to develop more of an interest in history – particularly learning about the history of different buildings or places.

Q. What are your goals/ambitions for the future?

I would certainly like to see Ghostcircle grow and expand more, and I'm excited to see how we can expand on the Ghostcircle TV series in different ways. I would also like to continue to work on my writing and have more articles published, and I hope to write and publish at least one book in the future – so watch this space!

Q. Do you feel there are any writers/authors who inspire you in your writing?

I would have to say the author who immediately comes to mind is Sir Arthur Conan Doyle. I love his style of writing and especially how he constructed his famous Sherlock Holmes series. I am still amazed at how he managed to construct his characters so well, with so much substance to them and so convincingly, that he had his readers believing these were real people rather than fictional characters. I think that because he made his characters, their storylines and traits so plausible, some people believed that they must have actually been living people (how else can a character be created so convincingly?), although I think in truth he simply based his characters on real people, taking inspiration from people around him. I have never before or since come across an author that has managed to do this so effectively or affect their readers in quite the same way, and it is something I hope I shall be able to do in my own writing.

Another author that inspires me is Agatha Christie. I am intrigued at how she constructed the plots to many of her murder mysteries and she also created some quite unique and memorable characters, such as Poirot. Recently, I have also read works written by Emma Donoghue, which has inspired me as she is extremely good at not just engaging the reader's interest and their mind, but also engaging them emotionally in her stories, which I think is always something a writer aims for in their work. Another modern author who I take inspiration from is J.K. Rowling. Looking at the way she started her writing career and the difficulty she initially had, and yet when her famous Harry Potter series was published, they were a sensation and she has made her success. This I find quite encouraging, as it is a reminder that no matter where you may be now, if you make the effort and persevere, you can achieve your dreams and make yourself successful.

Q. Are there any locations (already aired on TV) that stick out most to you and why?

This is a difficult question as each place we have investigated so far has been very memorable in its own way, and we have had unique phenomena and experiences at each location. Two places I really enjoyed investigating was the Castle Inn, in Warwickshire, as we had a lot of very clear EVP's, as well as hearing furniture moving in an empty room – which we knew was empty as we had just been in there. This was also the first time we were lucky enough to have Tracy Edwards, our gifted trance medium, come along where we were introduced to her guide Peter on camera. Another place that sticks out for me is Ross Castle. Here again we experienced a lot of phenomena, caught a lot of EVP's on camera, had a table move on its own while we were investigating one of the rooms and even heard somebody running down the tower stairs – twice! - Even though all of the team were in the same room (not to mention it would have been an amazing feat for any person to run down those tower steps at that speed!). Each location is a memorable experience and a privilege to film, and I hope we have many more to come.

Meet The Team – Karl Fallon

Q. When did you first realise you had a psychic gift?

When I was younger I actually had contact with some spirit guides from the age of three to about five years, but like a lot of young children who have this I lost contact with that side until my early 20's. I opened it up naturally again while trying some meditation exercises. When I say opened up, I mean that the ability was dormant within me and the conscious doorway needed to be unlocked again. What was most surprising at this time was that within in a month of opening up again, I saw two spirits over a weekly period at the end of my bed, in daylight.

Q. When did you start developing an interest in technology and filming?

I have always been interested in technology and computers as my university education was in Electronic Engineering. However, my interest in filming only started in late 2008/2009. I had to quickly get an understanding of using high production TV equipment. With the Ghostcircle psychic circles it was becoming necessary to capture and record any phenomena on sound and video. I didn't really have an idea how we were going to put this together as it has never been done before in this way, so it has taken quite a few years to figure out the best way to do this and has evolved into something quite amazing.

Q. As well as being the director, you are also in charge of the cameras and filming (most film crews have separate cameramen and directors). What unique challenge does this present?

It is extremely difficult to film Ghostcircle Productions, as we have no script and have very little control over what we do. I setup a scene and do some lighting but on some occasions I actually have to reduce the light, as it will destroy the energy around us. This means I have some grainy images or low light conditions to film in which is frustrating because I want to do it as best as I can. It's the complete opposite of a typical film shoot whereby you want full on lighting. It doesn't work like that with our mediumship. We are reliant on the spirit producing the phenomena, and I am amazed that we can turn up at a location and just get anything at all.

There are very few directors or cameramen who would put up with the same conditions, and I'm not just saying that. I'm directing, I'm filming, checking sound, adjusting lighting and listening to the conversation while also editing the scenes I will need later as I go along, because I know the shots that I will need to bring everything together when editing. Physical circles are extremely difficult to do as we shoot in a live, uncontrolled environment with external noises or weather outside, it's in semi-darkness, with people we haven't met before whom invariably chat and cough. Some people are also nervous, or could be afraid of the dark, or ghosts, but even with all this, we still manage to produce something. I'm always worried about bumping into or tripping over things, and I've the added difficulty of trying to get in close to get facial expressions, close ups, wide shots, and cutaways to split the scenes.

There are no second takes, this is always a one-time shoot as the energy comes in, it's there, and then it's gone. That's it. I have to capture it. I also cannot interrupt Patrick to do a retake shot I missed while he is talking to spirit. If I do this he invariably loses the connection. Believe me I have tried this once or twice and let's put it this way; it's easier to just carry on!

Q. What work do you do outside of Ghostcircle?

I work as an I.T (computer) consultant.

Q. What achievements do you have in relation to the work that you do?

I think I am the first person to capture the flower moving on camera and put it on TV. And I also know that we are the first to do physical mediumship using the photoplasm energy to do these psychic experiments, with members of the public. The people just turn up and see it in action. Ghostcircle has shown that photoplasm is a real phenomenon. We have repeated these psychic experiments with thousands of people following empirical methods; thus it is a repeatable experiment. And we get the same results again and again. It is not us that is seeing this, it is a wider audience most of whom have never believed in any of this before.

Q. What do you enjoy most about travelling and filming with Ghostcircle?

I enjoy it when it's done!! It's hard work most of the time, but we do get to see some amazing places and meet some interesting people too.

Q. Are there any locations (already aired on TV) that stick out to you and why?

I really enjoyed filming in Guernsey, it was a week of glorious sunshine and everything worked out really well. The filming went really smoothly and we had a good look around the Island. Filming in Rome and Italy was interesting too, but that's another story!

Q. Have you ever seen a ghost/spirit, and can you describe the experience?

I have seen many solid spirits, the first one being a young teenage girl standing at the end of my bed. She looked Indian in appearance, with very long dark hair. She disappeared after about 10 seconds. I also saw a monk in a white robe soon after. However, the strangest one I saw was a man made up of blue light who had a device about the size of a hand microphone, which he was moving up and down my body like something out of a sci-fi movie as I lay in bed. It had lots spikes sticking out of it. I looked up and saw he had a hood and robe on. He then realised that I was awake and shot back into the wall and disappeared. It was as if I wasn't supposed to see him. I have seen some very odd things around me when I wake up in the middle of the night. One morning I opened my eyes and saw a spider crawling over my pillow but when I tried to brush it off, my hand went through it. It was a ghostly spider. It then just faded away.

Q. What other interests or hobbies do you have outside of Ghostcircle?

I love keeping track of current affairs like news. I confess I am a real news hound and watch all the news channels or read the newspapers. I also like politics, history, art, antiques, filming, sport, science, gardening, space and technology, listening to podcasts, listening to the radio and of course, driving my car! It's nothing special but I do enjoy driving.

Q. What are your goals/ambitions for the future?

My main ambition is to keep filming Ghostcircle. I might also have a look at doing some film productions in the future. I have a few ideas for some movies at the moment.

Q. As the director/cameraman, what do you find most challenging about capturing paranormal phenomena (orbs/evp's etc.) on film, and how do you address these challenges?

As well as being the director, I am also a psychic medium too, and this also means that I can pick up on any spirits around us while filming. I'm good at sensing where the activity is while we are filming. Also, as I am part of the Ghostcircle group, I also find I get drained of energy not only physically, but also mentally. I am so mentally tired after filming, especially during a physical circle as the spirits around us also draw energy out of me too. Invariably I start yawning and my energy is drained during filming. As to capturing orbs and EVP's, well, I just hope I'm pointing the camera correctly and keeping it as still as possible. The rest is up to spirit around us. We seem to pick up lots of EVP's; I don't know why we get so many except it must be because of our harmony. We all work very well together. I'm not sure how it works, harmony is very important I know that. But things just happen around us although I can't explain how.

Meet The Team – Ben Clutton

(Jamie and Hannah next to Ben and Patrick outside the Vatican in Rome)

Q. When did you first realise you had a psychic gift?

Well, the supernatural and fantasy have always interested me, and as a child it was a great comfort to escape to a fantasy world. Therefore, when I started experiencing the paranormal for real, it intrigued me and I wanted to learn more. To answer the question; I still now sometimes doubt my abilities, but I have started coming to terms with my gift and very often surprise myself with the abilities I do have.

Q. When did you realise you had a unique affinity with plants/nature?

This is an easy one to answer! I've always had an affinity with nature, even as a young child. I would always have my head in the bushes and my hands in the dirt. I could have seriously pursued animal care or zoology, but gardening has always been my love and passion. Plants are better behaved than animals, so they won my attention! Plus their varying forms fascinate and enthral me.

Q. What do you participate in outside of Ghostcircle? (E.g.: gardening work/dog walking etc.)

I run my own Gardening/Dog walking business called Plants&Paws. This is, of course a combination of both private gardening and dog walking. The spring and summer are usually incredibly busy with gardening while the colder, wetter months are more devoted to dogs. Gardening is what interests me the most, while the dog walking adds a pleasant side line for the slower winter months – plus it's additional company for Luna, she's my dog! I may go on to do something else in the future, but who knows what the future holds.

Q. What achievements do you have in your work (courses/degrees etc.)?

I did five years of horticultural courses at the beautiful Bicton College in deepest Devon. I adored that place and learnt so much. I did a First Diploma in Horticulture, RHS courses in between, a National Diploma in Horticulture and then finished by doing my Degree in Horticulture. However, I have also learnt that in gardening, qualifications mean very little next to good experience.

Q. What do you enjoy most about travelling and filming with Ghostcircle?

Well there are so many things. We travel around the world an awful lot so we get to see lots of different places, and people do say you ought to travel around lots when you're young! History also really interests me, and travelling around with Ghostcircle you can't help but become absorbed with any local history with Patrick McNamara, as he knows so many interesting historical facts.

Q. Are there any locations (already aired on TV) that stick out most to you and why?

Schloss Erichsburg was definitely one to remember. We arrived on a sunny afternoon in June. The rambling, thickset castle was set in beautiful grounds run-a-mock with huge oriental poppies. It was wonderfully ruined and gothic. Very atmospheric, as well as being very haunted. The basement or dungeon area was absolutely awful, and incredibly creepy. There were some very sad tortured souls down there.

Q. Have you ever seen a ghost/spirit and can you describe your experience?

Oh yes many times. My earliest memory of seeing one was when I was a young child, and I probably didn't know what I saw at the time. It was a woman-like figure and I was playing on my own in my bedroom. I must have been about five or six years old. It disappeared as quickly as it came.

Since then, I have seen many, many, different spirit forms; and they still nearly always terrify me. I am getting better at it now. It's amazing what spirit can do for you.

Q. Have you ever seen fairies/nature spirits? Can you describe your experience?

Yes indeed I have. I was aware of them at a very young age, but my first proper encounter with fairies or nature spirits was about seven or eight years ago. It was in the heart of Kent on a friend's farm and all of the Ghostcircle team were there. Patrick McNamara, being the powerful medium that he is, placed a hand on my shoulder and showed me a cluster of blue cloud-like energy in the grass. The closer I looked, the more I saw. It was unmistakable. Fairies. I was in a state of shock and disbelief, but since then I've worked with different energies and I am aware of the spirits of trees, water spirits and all other earth elemental spirits. It's all energy, and it's amazing once you open yourself up to such things.

Q. What hobbies and interests do you have outside of Ghostcircle?

Well I am already an avid gardener, and this is my greatest passion. I spend most of my time dealing with plants and animals. However I also like to write, draw and occasionally paint. All the latter interests come and go with my emotions. Sometimes I write beautifully, at other times I struggle. It's the artist's bane. But with gardening I've found a happy medium between science and art. The ground is my canvas and the plants are my paint.

Q. So you have mentioned you also enjoy creative activities such as painting/writing. What kinds of things do like to paint or write about?

Well I keep a daily diary, which I think is very important. I also write down lots of notes. Letter writing is also a favoured past time of mine as I feel it is a lost art. I'm also going through an experimental phase with writing. I'm contemplating writing a novel, so we shall see how that goes. It's all in my head at the moment.

As for what I paint, that also varies. I like to paint landscapes and still life, which I know isn't as fashionable as it once was, but I still enjoy it. I nearly always use strong, bright colours, which also applies to my plant choices!

Q. You also have a lovely pet dog. Could you tell us more about her and does she also inspire your writing/painting?

Well I have a most beautiful Irish terrier called Luna. I consider her the love of my life. My day is completely governed by her routine, and I wouldn't have it any other way. I do believe having a dog is a lifestyle not just a pet. They consume you. I haven't consciously taken inspiration from her in my writing or painting that I've noticed, but she is a very important part of my life.

Q. What are your goals/ambitions for the future?

Well I don't consider myself to be a massively ambitious person, but one day I'd love to run my own Plant Nursery, specialising in Perennials and trees. I love plants and this is one of my dreams in life. I'm definitely a plants man!

Meet The Team – Patrick McNamara

Q. Have you always been able to communicate with spirits, and when did you first realise you had a gift in physical mediumship?

I have always been aware of spirit, and saw my fist spirit as a small boy. My grandmother was also a very good medium, and I was aware of objects moving around from a young age. I had been named after my two grand uncles who were her brothers, Patrick and Michael. Both brothers were killed by the same machine gun during the battle of The Somme. Their spirits appeared to my grandmother just after they had died, when they told her "we're dead, and we have come to say goodbye. We love you and we are ok."

When she tried to relate this to family and friends, she was admonished. However, three weeks later, a telegram arrived confirming they had both died, and at the exact same day that they had appeared to her. My grandmother could tell I was also gifted, and she used to say to me "People are afraid; you should not tell anyone, as they would not understand." As she said the words 'would not understand', the little side table in the room floated in the air and gently descended back down next to her. So you see, physical mediumship has always run in my family.

Q. Having developed your gift to such a degree, do you find this poses certain challenges in your everyday life? How do you deal with these challenges?

Challenges, yes most certainly! It can be quite off-putting at times when you see so much around you. There's the real physical world, and this intermingles (for me that is) with the spiritual world, It took me a long time to come to terms with the fact that I can see, hear, and feel spirit all the time. I had to learn how to handle my ability and close myself down. Even now, I sometimes still find it distressing when I can see illness or death in the people that I am close to.

I also find that I can affect electrical appliances around me. One of the great things about our team's mediumship at the moment, is that I can share the voices I am hearing – as we can all pick them up, which for me is quite reassuring. I sometimes have a strange effect on animals too; as they can sense the spirits and guides in my aura.

Q. What do you do outside of Ghostcircle? (Readings/paranormal advice etc.)

I used to do platform work for churches and gave a few private readings. However, now I tend to mostly confine myself to the experiments we do, as when people are able to see, feel and hear Spirit for themselves it is far more convincing than receiving clairvoyance. As we film most of our experiments, it also means that more people can be helped by seeing the reactions of everyday people and seeing the genuine mediumship from these experiments.

Q. What achievements do you have in relation to your mediumship and the work that you do?

I am happy that I have helped to train a group of young, enthusiastic mediums who are now working in light and getting amazing results in several forms of mediumship. That is an achievement in itself and very rewarding to see.

Q. What do you enjoy most about travelling/filming with Ghostcircle?

For me, it would simply be the joy of working with young mediums who enjoy all of the new experiences, forms of mediumship and new people that each film location brings. It is always fresh, new, and exciting to see the satisfaction and joy that each experiment brings. I think we have a very rewarding and satisfying occupation.

Q. Are there any locations (Already aired on TV) that stick out the most to you? Why?

This is very hard to answer because there have been so many interesting people and exciting places. We have been involved with so many wonderful people and places that it is hard to choose just one.

Q. Can you remember the first time you saw a ghost/spirit? Can you describe the experience?

As I mentioned earlier, I encountered my first spirit as a small boy. My mother had taken me to the bedroom for a nap, and I saw a spirit in the shape of a large skeleton with white hair and wearing a blue ring. My mother didn't see anything until she felt me tugging at her sleeve, whereupon she screamed, picked me up and ran from the room and over to next door, where her friend let her in after hearing her knocking.

After a brief chat, her friend related the history of our house. She told us that a man called Mr Joyce had lived there, and described him as being tall with blonde hair. She also confirmed that he used to wear a blue ring. Mr Joyce had died of a heart attack in the same room where we had seen him.

Q. **What other interests/hobbies do you have outside of Ghostcircle?**

I love music, fine art and paintings, history, fine foods and fine wines. If I have a maxim in life it is 'life is too short to drink cheap wine!'

Q. **I understand you have an interest in history and antiques. Do you find your psychic abilities add to your interest in this area? (E.g.: sensing past events etc.)**

I certainly think it does. You can get amazing psychometry from old objects, and it adds an extra bonus to being a collector as each piece has its own story to tell.

Q. What do you find most challenging about conducting physical mediumship experiments and producing phenomena for the purpose of filming? How do you address these challenges? (and indeed, does spirit guide you in this?)

I think the most challenging thing is working around other people's fears and expectations, as none of what we do can be predicted. It is always in the hands of spirit. As none of what we do is scripted, or planned; it also makes it very hard for the crew and cameraman to set anything up as we always do what spirit want us to – often with spectacular results. It is very hard work but also very rewarding.

Q. What goals and ambitions do you have for the future?

I would like Ghostcircle to be a global TV programme and organisation as I feel it is time that physical mediumship is brought into the light, which has already started to happen since the early part of the 20th century. Now, in the 21st century, we finally have the *technology to show the voice of spirit with a new and fresh approach so the whole world can hear and see the truth of spirit and the new understanding that is bridging the two worlds. At last we have not only the mediumship but also the means to prove to the world that there is **no** death.*

Meet The Team – Tracy Edwards

(Tracy with Eliza Packenham and Patrick in Tullynally Castle, Ireland)

Q. How did you first discover your psychic gift / start out in mediumship?

I have always been aware of an inner identity within myself that guides me since being a small girl of around five. When my mum died I was 19 and I coped quite well, but to me she hadn't gone. I still felt her present in my life, which seems strange. I loved her very much, but I went to work the next day. Life goes on and I don't believe in death just that we transcend the physical body. I realise I have always been a medium and psychic. It isn't learnt; we just listen to the inner part of us.

Q. Can you briefly explain what a 'trance medium' is and what this entails?

Trance mediumship involves a deep meditative state. There are many different levels:

- Entranced- when you can allow thoughts to be spoken through you and this is a light trance state.

- Trance – this state is a deeper trance state, which can involve a direct connection with spirit, either using trance healing or blending with spirit allowing a slightly deeper level of connection.

- Deep Trance – This is a much deeper level of trance where the medium is totally blended with the spirit energy allowing the voice to change. Some transfiguration may take place, and the medium will possibly not remember what the spirit has said. Blending with spirit takes time, patience and practice.

Q. Outside of Ghostcircle, what other events do you regularly participate in?

I work as a medium, deep trance medium, reiki master, and spiritual healer. I do like to help other people feel at peace with their lives. I teach all that I know on many levels. I offer private mediumship and psychic readings, trance and mediumship groups and I demonstrate to the public in clairvoyant evenings; anything up to an audience of 100 people. I regularly meditate and I sit and demonstrate deep trance to different groups of people.

Q. Do you have any achievements/qualifications in your field of work?

I am a Reiki Master and love working with the energy fields of people. I do consider myself to be an "energist" as I can read auric fields and a lot of my readings are about my clients' vibration. I am a spiritual response therapist, which means I help clear emotional blocks within the person and their energy fields. My early training as a medium included attending the Arthur Findlay College at Stansted Hall. I loved the weeks I spent there and the amazing teachers I had the honour of working with. I believe meditation and the ability to link with spirit is a natural process and one best developed with the medium and spirit, as there is no greater teacher. Wisdom is not measured by certificates it's measured by the heart, compassion and the ability to be true to the energy you're working with.

Q. What do you most enjoy about working with Ghostcircle?

I enjoy being part of a team of people who actually like each other, have a laugh and love working with spirit while proving time after time that life is eternal. We visit some amazing pubs, stately homes and different countries and some of the phenomenon we see is amazing. You never stop learning and expanding our consciousness as a group and as individuals.

Q. Have you ever seen a ghost/spirit, and could you describe the experience?

I have seen many spirits and they are a part of my everyday life. I perceive them as a normal daily experience. I don't always see them, sometimes I just feel them but I can describe the feeling of them and who they are etc. This is a more clairsentient feeling than a visual seeing. This has occurred since I was about five.

Q. What are your other interests and hobbies outside of mediumship?

I like to ride my horse – a beautiful thoroughbred mare. I regularly go to the gym, and I enjoy having a glass of wine with friends. I also love visiting new places, especially ones that are spiritual in nature.

Q. Would you be able to tell us a little more about the guide who works with you in trance? (Who they are, how you started working with them etc.)

I have a wonderful soul who works with me who has the most humbling energy, but don't be fooled he is very sharp! One day when sitting a friend of mine asked him what his name was and he replied: "which lifetime would you like, and does it really matter?" Apparently it did to my friend! They settled on Peter, a name that has stuck, and we refer to him today as Peter. The blending of energies is an amazing experience and to be fair it's innate in its nature. We all have an ability it just depends on how long you are prepared to sit and spend time blending with your own energy and that of spirit. It doesn't happen overnight, it takes time to develop.

Q. Do you communicate with your trance guide outside of your work in everyday life? How would you describe your relationship to them? (For example, do you view them as a close friend/work colleague etc.)?

I view Peter as the most wonderful soul who sometimes must get exasperated with me when I don't sit for long enough. His advice to others has helped give direction personally, spiritually and philosophically. I am very lucky to have an amazing friend who is always with me in my heart and, as he has explained many times, linear time is for humans. Spirit can be in many places at the same time, which is something I now understand.

Q. I understand you do healing work for people. Do you feel this has enhanced other areas of mediumship for you and how?

I think to offer others energy in the form of spiritual energy/healing is an act of kindness and working with this energy in its many forms is humbling. There are some amazing therapists who heal through thoughts, with energy, or maybe even just from being there for someone, as this in itself is healing. I love the energy of reiki, spiritual healing, angel healing, and emo trance; just to name but a few. It's not so much the therapy in my opinion but the person who resonates with the energy and gives it with love, kindness, humility and compassion. What greater gift can you give another person or animal?

Q. What are your goals/ambitions for the future?

I wish to follow my heart in this lifetime listening to the inner voice, and where ever that takes me is right for me. To help individuals listen to whom they are as a person/spirit and not who society or social conditioning has moulded them into being. I also want to teach peace and the importance of following your own inner wisdom.

Meet The Team – Jamie Wilkins

(Jamie Wilkins)

Q. How did you first discover your aptitude for classical music?

I've always had an interest in music, although this began with pop and modern music and in actual fact I started out listening to music through my grandad. It was only around the age of 11 when I started music lessons at school and having class piano lessons that I really developed my interest in learning the piano. It was these lessons in general which really started things off, when we learned how to play the black notes, called the black note march However, I have always felt drawn towards music and when I was in primary school I would be very curious about the school piano and other musical instruments. I used to love, as I still do, watching people play different musical instruments.

From there I bought books on the subject, and even bought myself a small keyboard to practice on. Whilst I was reading about playing the piano, I also discovered the art of writing music as I also used to compose my own little tunes – which also came in handy when learning to read music. My interest grew, and I started to devote all of my time to learning about music; how to read music and how to play the piano. However, at school, I still felt that nobody really took much notice of my talent or skills. It wasn't until my last year when the new head of music took me under her wing, she gave me private tutoring and helped me to complete the music exam. I also remember one concert pianist who used to sit at the piano with me and teach me the structure of music and how to play timing, giving me real encouragement and making me play in front of the class to show off what I could do. She is one of the people who really made a difference.

Q. I understand you were self-taught rather than having lessons to begin with. Were there any particular challenges you found with this?

There were quite a few challenges. The main one I imagine all self-taught people experience; that is that you tend to pick up a lot of "bad habits". One of these bad habits for me was slumping and/or leaning over the piano and not having the proper posture. Another one was not having the hands in the correct position to play the keys. It is more difficult when you are teaching yourself, as there is no one really who you can ask for tips or advice on how to do certain things. Yes, you can read through books, but they only give you a certain amount of information. Plus, it is one interpretation out of many, and if you don't understand what the author has said, you can't ask them to clarify the information!

You also need a lot of motivation and determination, as you do feel like giving up sometimes when things just do not make sense. Learning to read music didn't pose too many problems for me. All I did was get a blank piece of paper, copied the staves from the book and every day I would write the notes and their names on all of the lines, and after a while this becomes second nature. However, there are also different clefts to learn, such as the base cleft and tenor cleft, among others

- all with different notes, which you need to be aware of. I also had trouble learning timing with the piano.

It wasn't until I learned how to conduct that my timing became more accurate. When you are on your own playing the instrument without a tutor present, you can't really get an accurate sense of timing. This is where a metronome is really useful – I would even say mandatory – to anyone being self-taught. Being taught conducting, you learn to feel the beat; it has to come from within. So being an instrumentalist as well, you have to feel the beat before you start, and you then externalise this when playing. You also need to realise that the music has to 'breathe', and you have to breathe while playing too – which a lot of self-taught people don't do. It is more of a psychological process, as well as physically learning to play.

I think the most important thing is to know when to stop practising, as it is equally important to rest to allow your brain to process the information. Too much practice is just as bad as too little practice. You have to find a middle ground; if you stumble across a problem, just stop, then go back later to it later on. And nine times out of ten it will get better.

Q. Are there any music groups/orchestras etc. that you regularly enjoy participating in outside of Ghostcircle?

There are many orchestras which I regularly enjoy being a part of. I have become a part of the furniture in the conductor's orchestra, where I trained and continue to train as an orchestral conductor. Whilst I was training as a conductor, I really felt the need to go back to the Bassoon, as I had many lessons on this instrument many years ago. I also wanted to become a member of the orchestra to experience playing in an orchestral setting. With this in mind I brought a Bassoon, for at that time the bassoon section was very limited in lots of orchestras. I asked if I could sit in one day and play some sections. I have stayed there ever since. I also play for the Mary Ward Chamber Orchestra, of which I have been a member for over two years now. I was introduced to this orchestra by the flutist of the conductor's orchestra, to help out the Bassoon section.

I also hire myself out to various other orchestras. I have played Carmina Burana with the Water City orchestra, and have played many times with the Eynsfarn Sinfonia. I also play in a wind quintet once a month, where we go through a whole repertoire of works informally. We also premiered a Beethoven string quartet which I arranged specifically for this orchestra.

Previously, I have played the organ in a local church, and while playing the Bassoon many years ago, I played in a youth orchestra, which sparked my joy for playing orchestral music and was another inspiration for learning orchestral conducting. I also conducted the youth orchestra on one occasion, premiering a small orchestral work that I wrote.

Q. What would you say you enjoy the most about filming/travelling?

I think I would have to say it was meeting interesting new people, from minor royalty to Dutch television personalities, as well as people with interesting stories to tell. We have also seen many intriguing places of historical importance, and I enjoy getting the 'feel' of a place we visit. Being mediums we find our aura picks up on the atmosphere of an environment and you can almost 'feel' the history – it's almost as if the story of these places becomes a part of you. I also enjoy sampling the cuisine of each country we visit (especially cheesecakes!!). Most of all it is important for me not to follow the tourist beaten tracks, as I find it far more fulfilling exploring the real culture and less visited areas of a place.

Q. Are there any particular locations (already aired on TV) that stick out most to you? Why?

There are three places that stick out to me. The first has to be Schloss Moosham in Austria, due to magnificent size of the place along with the historical importance (it was the seat of government in the past). This was also the first place where we started to get good EVP's (electrical voice phenomena), and we helped to release a spirit, who thanked us by lighting our K2 meter (a meter which picks up on electromagnetic fields) as they were released. We also helped the owner to remove her fear of the place and the spirits that resided there. The second place that sticks out to me is Ross Castle in Ireland, where we had a door open up by itself, a table move in the tower and also, when we at the top of the tower, we heard a spirit running down the stairs on two occasions. Additionally we received excellent responses with our K2 meter. The general atmosphere there was very relaxed and a real family atmosphere – not what you would expect from a castle!

The third location that sticks out to me is The Castle Inn in Oxfordshire, as there was so much phenomena we experienced. I was pushed, and later on reviewing the evidence, there was a spirit EVP saying 'sorry I pushed you!' This was a great surprise – and it also confirms that it was a spirit that had pushed me.

Later on in one of the rooms I saw a lady standing by a bed, just for a split second, and I rushed over to where I had seen her to ask if she could make the lights on our K2 meter flash. At this, she made the meter flash quite quickly, before she vanished. This was more personal to me as I felt I needed confirmation that I had actually seen her. Also, we heard the sound of furniture being dragged around in a room above us, when nobody was there – we knew this as we had checked beforehand and locked the door.

The spirits were also answering questions for us using these 'dragging' sounds, and this was, we found, his preferred method of communication, as when we went up to the room where he was, he was reluctant to communicate with us. Peter (a spirit guide talking through Tracy Edwards in trance), predicted this would happen and told us there was a rather shy, well-to-do man waiting to communicate with us, but on his terms.

Q. Have you ever seen a ghost/spirit, and can you describe the experience?

The first experience I had was when I was 10 years old. It was midnight and I was lying in bed unable to sleep. At that time, I kept my door open and my bed was positioned so I could see onto the landing. All of a sudden, the air turned icy cold, and I felt a knot in my stomach. It was so cold I was able to see my breath, and I had goose bumps, but this change of temperature happened very suddenly (was not cold outside). I saw a solid figure that seemed as if it came out of the wall from the right of the landing where the stairs were, before walking past my door.

    The figure was solid enough to block the light in the doorway, and it was a perfect profile of a tall man. I couldn't see any features; it was just a pitch black shadow that slowly and purposefully walked from right to left, right past my door. I was in a state of shock and panic, and I called out to my nan to ask her if she had just walked up. In actual fact, she was in bed herself and simply told me to go back to sleep. She assumed that I had a nightmare. After that experience, the room went back to normal, and the temperature increased back to room temperature. I have since seen this figure on two more occasions, a couple of years apart. This is what initially got me interested in the paranormal. I have always believed in ghosts, but this was the first time I had seen one.

Q. What are your other interests/hobbies outside of Ghostcircle and music?

    I enjoy collecting Victorian and 1920's sheet music, and have acquired a small antique collection. I also enjoy computers and technology as I enjoy researching how things work. I've been collecting Victorian and Edwardian photographs, some of which have become very rare. Another favourite pastime of mine is reading about history and architecture. Other hobbies I enjoy include travelling (outside of our travels within Ghostcircle), collecting old and modern books, music scores, and musical instruments. Over the years I have gradually increased my collection of instruments, and now own a flute, an oboe, a clarinet, two bassoons, two trumpets, two violins, a trombone, a Victorian postal horn and a Georgian postal horn. I also enjoy cooking, good wine, and good food.

Q. What would you like to achieve for the future? Any goals/ambitions?

One of my goals is to conduct my own music in the Royal Albert Hall, and for the Ghostcircle team to get a FULL materialisation of a spirit on camera in light. I would also like to help as many people as we can through the work we are doing, to prove that there is life after death and that you CAN communicate with your loved ones who have passed away, you just need to know how.

Q. Are there any musical composers/musicians who you feel inspire you in your music? Are

there any composers/figures who you particularly admire?

The first musician I would say I admire is Beethoven, as he is the one who inspired me when I first started learning music. His inspiration was due to the range of emotions that he expresses in his music. He is often known for being loud and aggressive, but he can also be very subtle and absolutely sublime, such as in the Missa Solemnis and Symphony No. 6 (especially the 1st and last movement). Beethoven's mid to late string quartets are also my favourites as they show a much more personal and inward looking side of Beethoven.

The next person who has and continues to inspire me is the film composer Michael Kamen, who's music to the opening scene of Mr. Holland's Opus really encapsulates and romanticises how composers work and is also how I act and feel when writing music - especially when I'm writing a good tune or feel I am on the edge of a masterpiece. I have also caught Michael's voice as an EVP on a recording while I was conducting, so I truly believe that he inspires me with my music from spirit.

The most recent composer to inspire me is Mahler. His second symphony just seems to affect me every time I listen to it. The opening bars of the 1st movement always send shivers down my spine and touch me on a very deep level. As Mahler said, " Don't bother looking at the view – I have already composed it," He also said "I am hitting my head against the walls but the walls are giving way'" which is also very true for me too!

As far as conductors go, the conductors that inspire me are Simon Rattle; I love the way he works with his orchestra and treats them as individuals. I also like Marion Allsop who is very clear and gives a very clean performance. One of my favourite conductors of the past is Leonard Bernstein; I think he gives off such a wonderful energy and he wasn't afraid to be himself on the platform. Another conductor I admire from the past is Claudio Abbado, who conducted Bruckner's 4th symphony.

Q. I understand you also conduct as well as compose music. Which do you prefer/enjoy most, or do you enjoy them both equally?

They both go hand in hand. I am not just interested in conducting other composer's music; I also want to conduct my own music – which naturally means I have to compose it! When I am writing music, I always think to myself 'how am I going to conduct this?' Therefore both are equally as important to me. However, I do enjoy conducting, as I love the thrill of standing on a podium in front of an orchestra, not just leading, but creating music as a group and being able to mould and *shape the music as the conductor. Working with soloists is particularly fun!*

Q. Which instruments do you play? Are there any other instruments you would like to learn to play and do you have a favourite instrument?

I play the piano and the Bassoon, and I conduct. I also arrange, orchestrate and compose music. The instruments I would love to learn to play are the violin and the Cello, as well as the French horn. I have tried learning the violin, although all I was able to manage was a mere, sorrowful squeak! I have also tried learning the flute, which didn't go too well either. I have, on occasion, played the timpani in an orchestra – which is fun, as you can be really loud! However, it can be embarrassing if you play in the wrong place, as with the timpani the sound is unavoidable.

Greenways Farm

(The ancient Greenways Farm circa 1450)

One of the first places we investigated was a farmhouse in England that dates back to the mid 1400's. As we approached the old building, I felt my stomach turn with nervous anticipation. I was not yet a seasoned 'ghost hunter' per se, and I didn't know what to expect. It was clear that renovation work was in progress. The outside of the building still had the original wattle and daub plasterwork with the exterior with the original wooden beam supports.

You could almost feel the history that had saturated the very atmosphere of the place over the years, and it was thrilling to think that we would now be uncovering that history whilst hopefully unravelling some of the stories of its past. We were given a warm welcome by the owner of the farm Nick Jones, and I stuck as close as I could to Jamie for support as we sat by the original fireplace in the main reception room of the house. Coincidentally, this fireplace was also the only source of heat in the building. With a lack of central heating, a cold chill seemed to permeate the rest of the place, especially during the winter months which was the current season when we arrived.

As Patrick walked around with Nick Jones I listened curiously to Patrick recounting what he was sensing in the farm house. It was fascinating to see Nick Jones' reaction to what was being said and he corroborated a lot of what Patrick was saying as we went through the house. Patrick picked up on a man who had lived there many years before named Colin. He described Colin as being very proud to have owned a TV. Later on we discovered that a local neighbour recalled that there was a man who was named Colin who had indeed lived there. And intriguingly enough we were told that he had also been the first person in the area to own a TV, hence why he was so proud of this.

Another fantastic piece of evidence came when Patrick picked up on military connections relating to World War Two. The details he connected with were related to military machinery, aircraft, and an airstrip.

Later on after our investigation of the farm Nick told us later that as a result of what Patrick had sensed, he and a few others searched the farm with metal detectors and amazingly they actually unearthed aircraft parts in the surrounding fields. Nick also spoke to his neighbours who confirmed that there was a World War Two connection and said that during the war, a military operation had been based there. The neighbour told him that Greenways Farm had actually previously been called 'Searchlight Farm', because during these operations a searchlight battery had been installed in the nearby field. Therefore all of what Patrick had picked up on had been confirmed. Nick told us that he didn't know any of this beforehand.

Another character that Patrick picked up on was a man named Thomas who he felt had been a "dark" priest. He also sensed that he had worked with black magic, and had been involved with some witchcraft which he had used to exert control over people; in particular this was used on his relatives.

I really was amazed at this information. A part of your mind stubbornly tries insisting that there is no way this can happen, there is no way somebody's spirit can live on and even more, come back to relay this information to us. However, you can't deny what you are seeing with your own eyes. It is indeed very true, and very real. Based on what I had seen with Patrick's walk around, I was eager to see what Jamie, Ben and I would see on our ghost hunt later that evening.

Ben Clutton came along with us that night and he was another friend that I had met through Jamie. He seemed very shy and nervous when I first met him, although he clearly had a passion for plants – many a time all of us in the car have jumped after hearing Ben suddenly exclaim excitedly at some interesting plant, tree, or flower he had seen! He was also studying a horticulture course at college, and his sense of fun amused us all and made us smile.

We actually had a little free time before we were due to begin filming that evening, and so I managed to persuade Jamie to walk with me to the fields that bordered the farm and housed the few horses they kept there. Being an avid animal lover I naturally couldn't pass up the opportunity to acquaint myself with the animal life of the farm! As we approached the fence, a beautiful bay horse came trotting towards us, ears perked forward and a sparkle of curiosity in his big brown eyes. There was another smaller pony hesitating and standing a little behind the larger horse. However, after seeing us giving his friend some fuss, he gradually found enough courage to look around from behind his larger companion and also came forward for a little attention.

All too soon, it was time to head back to the house and get ready for the ghost hunt that awaited us. This was the first time I had ever actually participated in a ghost hunt, and instantly images crossed my mind from other paranormal programs of ghouls appearing out of nowhere and chasing us, things flying around the room with us running, screaming from the house.

In actual fact, the investigation turned out to be more subdued than I had first imagined. I must emphasise here that when I say *subdued*, I mean without any terrifying ghosts attacking the team members or false melodrama. By no means does it take away at all from the fascinating phenomenon that we actually pick up, it was simply not as terrifying as one would first imagine. To quote Ghostcircle director Karl Fallon: "we do interesting, not scary", and this couldn't be a truer quote. Our aim isn't to entertain people with sensationalism; it is simply to show that spirit world exists quite naturally around us while also bringing comfort, and reassurance to people, by showing real evidence that the spirit does live on. Life after death is a reality, and that loved ones who have passed before us are never far away.

To continue with our ghost hunt, as we ascended the stairs to the first floor (where a lot of the activity had been reported), Jamie, Ben and I looked at each other nervously and turned on our meters. There are generally two meters that we use. The first device is a simple voice recorder, which we use to pick up EVP's (electronic voice phenomenon). The second device we use is called a K2 meter, which detects electromagnetic fields (the substance the spirit's body is constructed of gives off an electromagnetic field which can be detected). Now, of course there are also electromagnetic fields in normal everyday life, so how would this indicate the presence of a spirit?

The answer seems to be that it's somehow due to the energy the spirits use. And when in the presence of a ghost or spirit you will usually see detect an energy field that is stronger than normal background ones around us. It could be unusual fluctuations in the electromagnetic field we don't really know, that's for science to figure out. A 'normal' electromagnetic energy caused for example by electricity, will stay at a consistent and constant level. This is shown on the meter by lights. If the lights 'flicker', this shows fluctuations in the energy it is detecting. When held next to an electrical wire/equipment, you will notice the light stays constant until the device is removed (as the energy is constant and steady), whereas if a spirit is producing this energy, you will often see the lights flicker, because of course the energy is fluctuating. If these fluctuations occur in the middle of a room or empty space, then this gives further evidence, because what else could possibly produce an electromagnetic field if there are no other devices, electric wires etc around?

After turning on our meters, we proceeded into the room where the spirit of a little girl called Rose was reported to haunt. In this room, there was a smaller cupboard. This cupboard was now used as storage but when Patrick had been walking around earlier he had picked up that this is where Rose had slept. So, this is where we began our investigation. As we entered into the room you could palpably feel the energy that was there. It was almost as if the air was alive and buzzing with static electricity.

I could also see a cloud of what appeared to be blue mist, which was strongest in the place where the little girl had slept. Jamie and Ben also confirmed they could sense the energy that was there. We placed the K2 meter into this cloud of blue mist we could see, and instantly the lights started flashing. All three of us looked at each other excitedly. Jamie asked if we were talking to Rose and once again the lights flashed in response.

We continued asking questions, and each time the spirit of Rose would make the lights flash if the answer was yes, or there would be no response on the K2 meter if the answer was no. I was thrilled with the responses we were getting, as this was the first time that we had actually come close to a full conversation with a spirit, with relevant responses to our questions. However, that soon came to an abrupt end as we caught the attention of another spirit.

As we were starting to become more confident talking to Rose and asking her more questions, I suddenly noticed that there was a different feeling to the room. The atmosphere and the energy around us had changed, and where it had at first felt light and pleasant, it now felt heavier and denser. It was almost like the feeling you get when dark clouds roll in on a sunny day and block the sunlight.

We tried asking Rose more questions, but this time there was no response at all. We then asked if there was anybody else in the room, to which we immediately got a response on the meter. My heart started pounding, as I instinctively felt this second spirit was not very pleasant. I then got the impression that this other spirit had a hold over poor Rose, which is why she was still here. I asked the spirit if he was holding this girl here, to which he immediately and boldly gave a definite response on the K2 meter to confirm.

I remembered the dark priest that Patrick had picked up on during his earlier walk around, and after asking if this was the spirit we were now speaking to, we again received an affirmative response on the meter. I don't think Rose was necessarily scared of this priest; it was more that the priest was clearly still trying to keep and exert control in any way he could. Jamie, Ben and I all now felt uncomfortable in this room. We did not want to continue a conversation with this priest, this man, and so we decided to carry on investigating to see if we could re-establish contact with Rose.

We left that room and moved in the hallway outside. Things started happening again when we started investigating the room at the end of the hallway. It seems that we had made contact with another pleasant spirit of an old lady who we felt worked there. She informed us through responses to different questions we asked, that she was actually helping to protect Rose. She then revealed that where we were standing and talking to her it was in fact a portal of some kind that was used by Spirits to move between our world and theirs.

We could still feel the presence of the dark priest, but it was almost as though a type of 'force field' was keeping him at bay, because all three of us sensed that he was staying at the opposite end of the room to us. Throughout all of this I remember feeling absolutely fascinated. It was the first time I had actually seen evidence that we could have intelligent conversations with spirits, receiving relevant answers to our questions.

After we had completed our ghost hunt, it was time for the physical circle experiment. I have already explained in the previous chapter the format that is used in these circles, and thus the experiment was set up in this way. Old Toby, Nick Jones' faithful labrado, came loping over from one person to the next lapping up all of the attention he received. He was ever hopeful for any leftover sausage treats from the kitchen, or from any of us! Looking up at you with his smiling expression, it was hard not to adore this gentle dog. Once we had finished setting everything up, Toby was taken out of the room and we started the circle.

When it came to the first time we experienced the flower moving Ben's reaction was amazing. He was the first to experience it and we did this in Greenways farm and captured it on camera. The flower was turning a complete 360 degrees in his hand, and this is the first time that Ben had seen this, or any of us. He was clearly astounded by it and I don't think he was sure if he could believe his own eyes, but it was most definitely real as every one of us there was seeing the same thing. It moved to fast and clear that it's was quite simply stunning. And we captured it on our video camera.

(The flower moving in Ben's hand in the psychic circle)

After we finished the physical circle we packed everything away we headed out to the car. All of a sudden outside we all stopped. We could hear a bell, like a church or a tower bell ringing. I was confused as I hadn't remembered seeing any churches or towers or anything else of the sort nearby. We discussed with Nick Jones what we all had heard, and we discovered that at one time there had actually been a bell tower by the farm. It was eerie in a way as you could very clearly hear the ghostly sound of the bell echoing through the night, as though the farm itself remembered the bell tower that had once been there.

Nick Jones also pointed something else out to us. Patrick had picked up earlier on a windmill that had previously stood in one of the fields of the farm. There were no windmills currently there now, but after talking to his neighbours, Nick confirmed from an old lady nearby who remembered that indeed at one time there had been a windmill, and he directed our attention to a certain area of the field. There, we could clearly see what appeared to be a hill, or mound, which interrupted the otherwise relatively flat grass surface of the field. We then realised that this is actually where the previous foundations of the windmill had been.

It was amazing to think that we were able to tap into all of this history, and it was the first evidence I had seen that an environment, even the land itself can be imbued with past memories; imprints of what has happend before. It brings about a sense of awe and a new respect for anything historical. I was sad to leave that interesting place, but was also excited at what may lay ahead in the future. If our investigation here had been this interesting, I was excited to find out what else we could discover.

Binnenveld House

(Patrick with Johan Vlemmix in his extremely haunted house)

Binnenveld house is a beautiful spacious old manor house located in the centre of the town of Huissen which is located in the Netherlands or Holland as we like to call it. It was the first time I had been abroad and so this particular trip for me was going to be packed with new and exciting experiences. I found Holland to be a very picturesque country with very friendly and welcoming people. The hustle and bustle of towns such as Delft captivated me. Staying in Delft which is a university town, I found the energy in the town so uplifting. There was a real buzz and liveliness probably helped by all the students on their bikes flying around, but it filled me with great excitement.

While staying in Delft, we visited the monthly and wonderful antique market held there. The market went on for miles with a variety of different stalls selling lots of intriguing items. I ended up buying some salt and peppershakers to take home to my grandmother. They were made of delft china which she absolutely loved. They were made in the shape of a windmill (photographing windmills had been a favoured hobby of my grandad), and so they were the perfect gift for her. It also amazed me in Holland seeing for the first time the amount of bicycles and cyclists. Everywhere you turned there were people of all ages darting along the roads or simply enjoying a ride together. Indeed, I soon found that when crossing the road in Holland it's the cyclists you often need to double check for more than the cars!

We also visited the Keukenhof Flower Festival. Ben being an avid plant lover and gardener, couldn't wait to get there! For anybody who has ever been to this festival before, I am sure will probably agree with me, that it is one of the most extraordinary places in the world. Flowers and tulips of every shape, size and colour adorned the gardens in the most delightful displays that highlighted their beauty. There was also a brilliant energy exuded by the flowers themselves. If you have ever been in a place where immediately you've felt nothing but joy and happiness simply from your surroundings, then this is probably in part due to the energy, or the vibration exuding from that place. For psychics, or people who are a bit more sensitive, this feeling is felt with much more intensity. I could sense something that I would describe as a "gentle humming sensation" that literally filled the air around us. There was such a sweet scent of perfume from each flower that subtly added to the pleasant feelings with the beautiful sight of flowers everywhere. The sun was out and we had a band playing lots of merry tunes in the background. It is no exaggeration to say the Keukenhof Flower festival was nothing short of a haven where people could relax and enjoy their surroundings and each other's company.

(Keukenhof flower festival)

The next day we travelled Huissen to see the owner of the house that we were investigating. His name was Johan Vlemmix, and he was a Dutch radio and TV star. Apart from being a wonderful and welcoming host, he was a very eccentric and charismatic man. It is impossible not to respond to his exuberant energy, and all of us in the team liked him instantly. Johan explained to us that he usually purchases and restores haunted old buildings. When we arrived he had been building a full size bar in which to hold Royal dinners and parties. He is also a friend of the Dutch Royal family which he adores. Johan even told us he had been present at the Dutch King's crowning, and showed us a tattoo that he had on his foot of a royal crown which he had done especially for the Kings coronation. He even revealed to us that he had given the King a Porsche Turbo as a coronation present! We were also introduced to his friend Andrea Ladida. Andrea was helping Johan in his ventures with the house. She was a charming lady and like Johan very welcoming, She was more reserved than her eccentric friend Johan. Andrea had also had her own share of paranormal experiences in the house, which included sensing a presence on the first floor landing and feeling as though somebody is watching. She also worked as a photographer and told us about the time that as she was trying to compose a particular photograph one day upstairs, she was slowly walking backwards trying to find the best camera view, when she felt as though she had bumped into something, or someone. When she turned around, however, nothing was there. But she felt that there was a solid presence there.

Before starting our investigation, Johan explained to us how he had come into possession of the house, as this had an interesting story to it to say the least! He told us that he believed the place was cursed, and then, in his effervescent way, proceeded to explain why. He originally brought the house with the intention of using it to run a ghost programme on his 24 hour TV channel.

However, from the moment he first took an interest in the property, a strange string of misfortunes seemed to plague him. Firstly, just as he set out to view the house his GPS malfunctioned on the way and he got lost. He then bought a map to look up the directions; only to find that the exact map pages he needed were missing from the book. When he finally started on his way there, his tyre burst quite violently. And, while he was getting the tyre fixed, another car came speeding down the road and nearly knocked him over. Due to this string of misfortunes he ended up arriving for the appointment a full six hours late. Amazingly, undeterred in spite of these apparent warning signs, Johan bought the house, and subsequently suffered a relationship breakup, loss of money, a business failure, not to mention various health problems. Johan told us that he also had a total of fifteen accidents in the house some of which he needed hospital treatment; including a broken leg. It is no wonder then that he quickly drew the conclusion that the house was decidedly cursed with bad luck! Oh yes, there was also an incident when somebody tried to burn the house down.

(Binnenveld House)

Johan then went on to explain some of the paranormal phenomenon that he had experienced. As mentioned before, one of Johan's hobbies was restoring old haunted houses. He was in the process of renovating Binnenveld House when we filmed there, and I remember one particular incident he recounted to us about a drill spontaneously switching itself on. This drill wasn't only switched off at the time; it was actually *unplugged* from the wall socket. There was also a wealth of other poltergeist activity, and loud noises had been heard during the night, as though someone was running around. The noises were so loud that Johan thought there were intruders at first, or that people were accessing his property. As a result of this activity he built a fence around the house and placed new locks on the doors.

However, the noises continued, and there was never any obvious physical cause found.

I was fascinated just listening to him recount his stories. It was by far one of the most active places I had thus far encountered. During the interview with Johan, Patrick told us some of the things he was picking up on in the house and the property. There were German soldiers present and he sensed that they had been billeted there. He also saw the face of a girl in one of the upper floor windows looking out when he was outside in the garden. Perhaps one of the most strangest incidents he re-counted, was that he even sensed the spirit of a cow when we walked around to the back of the house (there was a farm there and a housing estate has been built around it), which just goes to show you can never really tell what you will discover…it can be surprising! All of this information was corroborated as Johan first confirmed that a previous family had to move out of the house as German soldiers were billeted there, corroborating the military connections Patrick was sensing, and he also said that before being built on the area had been pastureland, which is maybe why Patrick sensed the cow! He even confirmed that a lady who had been pregnant had died there, which could confirm the girl that was seen in the upper floor window.

Additionally, Patrick gave Johan a reading, which I could tell captivated his interest even further. He picked up on a lot of personal connections for Johan in relation to his family, and at one point Patrick mentioned he was seeing fireplaces, whereupon Johan confirmed this by saying a man had previously lived in the house with his brother, and they had indeed built fireplaces there. Another interesting piece of information was revealed when Patrick said he could sense the date of an anniversary coming up. At the mention of this Johan then informed us that on the 4th May, the people of Holland all pay their respects to loved ones who have passed. None of the Ghostcircle team were aware of this before filming. Once the interview was over we then proceeded into the house to continue our investigation.

    Most of the investigation inside the house was conducted alongside Andrea, who gave the grand tour of the rooms while Patrick recounted what he was sensing. It was obvious right from the outset that the place was very actively haunted. While we walked around filming, we could hear voices talking and commenting on what was being said. We even heard someone singing at one point! Thinking it was somebody else in the house, we went to ask them to be quiet while we were filming, only to discover there was nobody there.

    In one of the rooms we filmed in, there were two chandeliers. While Patrick was explaining what he was picking up on, we noticed that one of the chandeliers started swinging. Admittedly, you would first naturally look for an open window to see if a breeze was moving it, or any other logical explanation. However, I mentioned that there were two chandeliers in this particular room. The second chandelier was actually closer to the window, which in fact was closed, and was not moving or swinging at all which convinced all of us that this was clearly evidence of some paranormal activity.

In one of the other rooms, Patrick again picked up on a German soldier. He also mentioned that this soldier kept drawing his attention to one of the large cupboards, except that instead of a cupboard, he was seeing a wall with a map that this soldier kept pacing in front of and looking at. This also tied in with the military connections that Patrick was sensing in the grounds outside the house.

Andrea then led us into what was known as the children's room. We could see a number of children's toys placed about the room. However, once there you got the distinct impression of feeling dizzy as soon as you stepped in. Patrick went on to explain that he sensed a lady that had passed in the room after a long illness, which accounts for the dizziness that people felt upon entering this room, and yet again he picked up on another German soldier!

About half way through our tour, Johan re-joined us in walking around the house. Perhaps the strangest room we encountered was the basement. During the tour, as Johan showed us this room, all of us were quite surprised to see a number of coffins before us. Johan saw our nervous, if not quizzical expressions, and smiled as he lifted open one of the lids. Imagine our surprise when we saw the coffin was actually filled with bottles of champagne! These coffins, we learned, were kept for two purposes; the first being due to Johan's television connections and filming for programmes, and the second was cold storage for the champagne for when Johan entertained guests or held parties, so that there was certainly never any shortage of drinks! He even gave us a demonstration for the camera and laid down in one of the coffins, with each of us looking on with equal amounts of fascination and amusement.

(The Coffins in the basement. They were not used!)

Next, we headed to the upper levels of the house and to the attic, which I have to admit wasn't as entertaining. None of us felt at all comfortable in this room. I for one kept feeling as though there was something standing behind us and closely watching. There was a distinct feeling of ill ease that felt threatening and made me want to get out of that room as quickly as possible. Patrick then explained that he was picking up on a man with a nasty temperament, who had not been very pleasant with children. He also picked up on a second man in this room, again who was also not very pleasant and Patrick felt that he had hung himself in there.

When we reached the room that Johan was currently using to sleep in, we uncovered yet more paranormal activity. Johan said to us that there was a man in his neighbourhood that had used dowsing rods. On one occasion this man had investigated the house using dowsing and while dowsing in this particular room, he was physically pulled forward, seemingly by a spirit or entity. The man then proceeded to say that it was probably better not to sleep in that room! Johan told us that he had at one point almost been trapped in this particular room. There were sliding doors that are quite easy to move and open, and the doors have no locks on them. However, one day when Johan was in this room, he tried to open them and found that he couldn't. Try as he might, he just couldn't move or open them at all.

After Patrick had finished his investigation of each room, we then had a bit of a break before we went back to filming the circle. I mentioned earlier that Johan was a friend of the Dutch Royal family. Johan showed us a special cheese that had been made specifically for the crowning of the King, and during our break we had the privilege of being offered a sample of this cheese to eat along with a well appreciated cup of tea!

Once everything was ready, we then began our circle. This time we did not have a tent as we normally do. Instead, Patrick began as always by building the energy within the circle, and asking Johan what he was seeing and experiencing. He was naturally very perceptive and open minded, and didn't scare easily, which always makes it easier for us as mediums to work. In my experience I have seen that if you have somebody who is not willing to keep an open mind, or who is scared, it makes it very difficult sometimes for spirit to work. If somebody stubbornly refuses to accept even the possibility of paranormal phenomena, even though they are confronted with tangible evidence and cannot otherwise provide an explanation for what is occurring, then in some respects you are coming up against a brick wall. It is like the saying 'there is none so blind than those who will not see'.

Conversely, if somebody even one person in the group is worried or fearful, then again it limits what spirit can do. The simple reason for this limitation is that most spirits never actually want to frighten people, and consequently if they know somebody is nervous they will not go beyond a certain point in order to avoid scaring them.

This is why I say that we were fortunate to be working with Johan. He was both open minded and more fascinated than fearful, and so this in turn made it easier when it came to showing him the energy that was built within the psychic circle we did with him.

Overall, our trip to Holland and Binnenveld house was fascinating. It was packed with lots of wonderful sights, some very intriguing paranormal phenomena, and of course the interesting people like Johan and Andrea. I was immensely glad to have met Johan. He was such a lively and exuberant character and all of us in the team found it very easy to talk to him, and thoroughly enjoyed his company. So we packed the car and hit the road driving through the picturesque Dutch towns and countryside with fond memories of the beautiful flowers of Keukenhof behind us we headed off onto our next adventure, optimistic of more wonderful places and experiences to come.

(Patrick and Johan upstairs during the Interview)

(Johan during the physical experiment we did with him)

Schloss Erichsburg

(Ben, Jamie, and myself 'concentrating' on the top floor of Schloss Erichsburg)

Following our adventures in Holland, our next investigation took us into Germany and the quaint borough of Dassel. Our destination was the grand, and very old Erichsburg Castle, a 16th century lowland castle owned by an intelligent airline pilot called Manfred Schneider. The building in itself, although at present largely in a state of disrepair, was certainly very impressive, simply by its vast size and the beautiful grounds that surrounded it. This was enhanced even more by the weather, with the bright sun highlighting the beauty of the landscape. As we approached the Manor that stood to the side of the main castle, my eye was drawn to the grounds surrounding the edge of the property. I could see long grass with flowers and trees that seemed to stretch back further than I could immediately see, not to mention the exciting anticipation of a wealth of paranormal phenomena that beckoned from the castle building, and I was curious to explore this grand place.

As I stepped out of the car, a succession of barks and yelps interrupted my thoughts, and I turned around just in time to see a Great Dane loping towards me, followed by his companion, who looked to be a Labrador/Alsatian cross. A third smaller terrier dog yelped at us from the vantage point of a balcony. My natural fondness for animals contrasted briefly with the slight wariness I felt from the dog's sheer size and not knowing his temperament, especially being of a petite build myself. Ben was clearly far less nervous and boldly approached the huge dog. I mused to myself how this courage often seemed to desert him when it came to the paranormal and the world beyond!

However, it was soon apparent that he was friendly enough, and once he ascertained that these strange unexpected visitors to his home posed no threat (it seemed these animals were kept at least in part to guard the property), they continued to ramble amiably throughout the grounds, approaching us occasionally for a bit of fuss and attention before rambling off again.

After initial introductions, Manfred explained to us that he was in the process of restoring the Castle. In a private interview with Patrick he explained that it was his intention to turn the building into a museum, preserving some of the original features of this historical place. Patrick then mentioned he was picking up that there seemed to be a floor missing. Amazingly, Manfred then confirmed this and told us that due to the top floor of the building being in such disrepair and collapsing, this naturally made it too dangerous, and so that level was removed. This restoration is something I really admired him doing, not least because other buildings in a similar condition so often are deemed too tedious and costly to repair and so are demolished with the land then being used for other purposes. Interestingly, Patrick also picked up on what he described as a crest with an image of a bird on it, similar to a coat of arms. At first, we weren't entirely sure what exactly this was, although we found later on while walking through the castle the exact coat of arms that Patrick had seen on the wall above one of the doorways of the castle. The detail was exactly as he had seen, even down to the blue background that the bird was depicted against. Considering we had as always come to this place with no knowledge of the castle or its history, it was certainly an amazing piece of confirmation!

While Karl was working on taking some outside camera shots and generally setting up things, Ben, Jamie and I explored the massive grounds surrounding the Schloss. Manfred had explained to us that he hosted various special events in the grounds of the castle, things such as concerts and various fairs. Looking at the beautiful landscape that surrounded us it was not difficult to see why you could these events here.

(Schloss Erichsburg Forest)

The grounds stretched far back behind the Castle manor. As we explored the area it felt almost as if we were in a fairy tale forest; with the long grass, the wild flowers, numerous trees and also a huge pond which we came across towards the back of the property. Ben was clearly in his element as he led the way, while Jamie and I stuck close together as always, holding hands as we enjoyed this wonderful, atmospheric place.

Although we were enjoying the grounds and historical buildings, we were not solely exploring the grounds for pleasure alone. We were also opening our senses psychically in order to see what we could also sense from the place. Each of us picked up various things, and I remember myself sensing that there had been a fire. It was almost as if I could see the flames, and this information I was to learn later on, would reveal its significance. When I relay information that I am picking up, the question is often asked, "Well how do you sense this information?" To answer this, it is important to understand that psychics and mediums can pick up on information in a variety of ways, including clairvoyance (seeing visions or images), clairaudience (hearing sounds/words), clairsentience (having gut feelings or picking up on emotions), and so on. Some of these methods can also be combined, for example, you may 'see' pictures or images, and you may also feel an emotion that is related to this.

When I was sensing the fire, the best way I can describe it is to say that as I looked around at my surroundings, it almost looked as though the grounds *were actually* on fire. I could still see the trees, the grass, the flowers, but the images of the flames almost seemed to be superimposed over the top of this. It wasn't a very strong vision, but I definitely felt that this was something that had happened here at some point.

Patrick then conducted his walk around with Manfred recounting what he could sense from the grounds. One of the first things Patrick mentioned was having the sense of lots of horses. Manfred then confirmed that the castle had been used during the war and that cavalry horses had been bred there. He mentioned at one time there had actually been something in the region of 5000 horses there, which just gives an idea of the scale of its importance. Patrick also picked up on armoury and war equipment, which again Manfred confirmed, showing the castle clearly had a lot of significance in the 30 year's war.

When we headed into the cellar of the castle, you were immediately overcome with a feeling of dread. Naturally a place such as a castle cellar may be likely to induce such feelings due to the very atmosphere, but it was more than that. Patrick also mentioned here that he was picking up on a lot of cruel things taking place, including prisoners being tortured and even one prisoner who seemed to have managed to seize an opportunity to murder the guard that had been responsible for his suffering. Even more eerily, while Patrick was explaining this gentleman he was picking up on to the camera, an orb appeared and flew towards where Patrick was standing, seemingly somehow drawn in by Patrick himself. We also caught this on the film, as well as a voice around the same time which sounded like it was saying "coming back", both giving us an added piece of great confirmation as it all tied everything in with what Patrick was picking up. If you were to glance up at the ceiling of the basement, you could even see where the trap door would have been that would have been used to throw convicted prisoners down into the Cellar.

(The old trap doorway into the cellar – with later hook?)

As we continued on our tour of the castle, it became apparent that it had once been used as a courthouse, with the lower levels being used as a judging room, and the upper floors being strictly for the use of the upper classes where dinners and parties would have been held. However, Manfred had a slight surprise in store for us as he mentioned there was a particular area that he wanted Patrick to investigate, to see what he could pick up on. He led us to a stone passageway with a stairwell that spiralled upwards.

Patrick immediately picked up on a small dog that was there, although even more than this, he picked up on the spirit of a little boy who had fallen down the stairs to his death. Patrick described the boy as being content and happy, and said that his death had been instantaneous, and so he had not suffered. Patrick also asked me if I was able to sense anything in this area. I could certainly sense the spirit dog that he had picked up on. However to my surprise, instead of sensing the little boy, once again I picked up on fire. This time the vision was stronger than when I had been outside and I was even more surprised when Manfred confirmed that indeed there had been a fire there. When we looked back through the film footage later, we also caught a great EVP from the little boy, stating in a child's voice that he was seven years old (which Patrick had also accurately picked up on), so once again we received fantastic confirmation.

We then moved further on into the castle, and as we started to reach the higher floors, Patrick started to pick up on the strong presence of a lady who he described as having a large, flamboyant hairstyle, and who was authoritative over some of the other men who would have been there at one time. She certainly seemed to be a lady who made her presence known to people there and ran the place! There was a pleasant surprise as we passed through one of the main rooms, when we saw a pair of swifts flitting and darting above our heads and giving loud calls as we filmed below them. Manfred explained to us that these two birds were breeding here. They had been seen in this same place the previous year and so had obviously returned to the same breeding site. By madly flying and darting above our heads, they were clearly trying to distract us away from where their nest was, as they would with predators in the wild, although I have to say it was delightful to see this impromptu flight display. These charming little birds and their character somehow seemed to add to the grand appeal of the Castle. As we went along, Manfred was also explaining to us that he sometimes allowed paranormal groups into the castle to investigate. One of the common things that these paranormal groups reported was that a spirit known as 'The Lady In White' haunted the castle.

As we moved from room to room, we found more and more interesting pieces of evidence that added to the whole story of the castle, including a man that wandered on one of the upper floors who liked to assert himself over people, and there was even a church where we uncovered the story of a clergyman who hanged himself from the beams of the church doorway. Each room had a unique story to tell, and it is probably among one of the most interesting places we have investigated.

When the time came for Jamie, Ben, and I to do our ghost hunt, it was decided amongst all of us that we would actually do this during the day while it was still light for the simple reason that it was just too dangerous to explore this castle in the dark due to the state of disrepair. Looking back, this was actually an enormous turning point for our team. EVP's and other phenomena can be notoriously difficult to achieve in light as white light actually destroys the energy that is being created. This is why most groups conduct their experiments in the dark (aside from the obvious atmospheric effect).

In Ghostcircle, we do not do our experiments in darkness to pitch black but we rather use red and blue lights so people can see exactly what is going on. Although the vibration of white light can destroy the energy, red and blue light, used in the right way, does not. In fact, red light, as I have seen from the many circles we have done, helps the physical energy to build, and so this is why we are able to use this. The only difficulty is that you have to get the right level of lighting. Too bright, and it can be counterproductive, and possibly start destroying the energy that is there, and too little, and it can make it even more difficult to actually build the energy for the spirits to use. However, once you have the correct level of lighting the benefits are two-fold. It is easier for the spirits to use the energy to create physical phenomena, and the presence of the lights also allows all of the circle sitters present to fully see everything that is going on, meaning that there are no illusions or tricks. The lighting also means that we are able to capture and record the phenomena on camera, so if there was to be any doubt about an incident (we don't take every incident or occurrence as being paranormal), all you would need to do is rewind the tape and look back at it to see the proof, thus further emphasising the point that there are no illusions or tricks in our investigations.

Although I have digressed slightly, I feel it is important to explain these details, as my hope is that it will help people to understand the paranormal and what we do, and also take away a lot of the fear associated with it and instead replace that fear with interest and curiosity combined with a willingness to keep an open mind. Returning back to our ghost hunt; as I mentioned previously, due to the extensive dereliction in parts of the building we conducted our investigation in the daylight hours.

This was the first time we had conducted our investigation in this way, and I was wondering how it would alter things, and even whether we would be able to get anything at all due to the reasons I have just outlined on how light affects the energy that is created. Still, we took a deep breath, and headed together towards the basement to see what we could find.

As it turned out, my initial fears proved to be unfounded as the ghost hunt went better than any of us could have expected. In the cellar we caught a lot of EVP's including a dog barking and spirits responding to our questions in German! At one point, we attempted to talk to the spirit of the prisoner that Patrick had first picked up on. We asked if he could tell us what happened to him, and when we replayed the tape you could hear the words 'He bonds with her', and I immediately felt sick as the Spirit was entering or 'bonding' with my aura. Another example was when we picked up on the spirit of a lady. I asked her if she had any children, and again when replaying the tape we heard first the word 'Kinder' (the German word for children), then the words 'no children'. Some of the responses we got were spoken in English, but even then you could clearly make out a German accent in the voices. For us, the fact that we were getting relevant responses to the questions we were asking was further proof that what we was doing was real. Not only is the spirit world a very real reality, but they are able to see, listen, and understand what we are saying and give us appropriate responses to our questions.

Some people find this quite surprising, but for me, it is simply common sense. Spirits, as we so term them, are still just like you or me. When somebody dies, their spirit body is separated from their physical body, but the person is exactly the same. Their personality, their likes and dislikes, their sense of humour... they are exactly the same person they were one minute after death as they were one minute before, therefore why should it then be so surprising that they can talk to us and communicate with us just as we who are living communicate with each other?

As well as capturing these great EVP's, I think the most memorable part of this investigation was the flower movement. Even though it was in daylight we decided to try the flower experiment anyway just to see what would happen. As it turned out we ended up getting some of the best results we have ever had with the flower movement in this experiment! Ben held the flower between his fingers, just as we normally do in our physical circles, while Jamie and I asked spirit to help us turn the flowers. Once again, we could clearly see the clouds of energy surrounding the flowers, and Ben mentioned that he felt as if somebody was holding his shoulder, passing energy through him. It was then that the flower started to turn; and what was amazing was that the flower must have completed about at least three full 360-degree turns while we were filming. I think it's safe to say we were all thrilled and absolutely speechless. Even I was a little dubious at first as to whether we would get any good results in broad daylight, but once again I was proven wrong! It just goes to show that in the spirit world you should never say 'never'.

(Ben and I excitedly watch the flower move 360 degrees)

Our exciting visit here was then concluded at the end by a rare treat. If you were to climb the ancient stone stairwell even further after passing the chapel I had mentioned before you would enter the bell tower. Manfred very kindly agreed to sound the bell for us, so that we may have this to add to our camera footage. Naturally, all of us were very excited at this, although for safety reasons and due to space constraint only Karl and Patrick followed Manfred to the tower in order to film the impressive castle Bell. Jamie, Ben, and myself waited on the floor below where the chapel was, and listened to the impressive grand sound of the peal of the bell, which undoubtedly could be heard for miles. I really don't think our visit there could have been concluded any better!

I mentioned earlier that our decision on this occasion to conduct our experiment in daylight was a turning point for the Ghostcircle team – and it was. Now, with such good results, this opened up a wider avenue for us to work with in our investigations. Of course, it is still easier to conduct our experiments in the dark with red and blue lights, due to the reasons outlined earlier, but we were no longer completely reliant on this as a factor anymore. We had built the energy within our team to such a level that we were now able to get these results in daylight. I was particularly pleased about this, as it would allow people to see the evidence and phenomena we capture much more clearly, and my hope is that as it can be repeated again and again, and now even in differing conditions and locations, that this will further help to open people's minds to the reality of life after death.

Schloss Moosham

(Theresita with Patrick showing him round the castle's hundreds of rooms)

Feeling jubilant and optimistic after our last successful investigation and enlightening discovery of our ability to work in light, our travels next took us across the German border into Austria. This time our destination was the famous Schloss Moosham near Salzburg, owned and managed by the wonderful Theresita Khan, daughter of the count and countess Wilczek.

When we first arrived at the Schloss, we saw in front of us a series of cabins which we later realised were used as accommodation for guests. Then we turned around, and were greeted by the magnificent sight of the castle. It really was like seeing a castle out of a film (we later discovered that this castle and its grounds *had* been used as film sets in the past by various film producers). A drawbridge led the way across to the castle courtyard, and beyond that the entrance was to the castle itself. There were hundreds of rooms in this castle and unfortunately it was just too large for us to investigate the entire castle during our visit there. I think it would have probably taken weeks to properly investigate each room in the castle! Some of the castle's main features included a torture room and judging room, both of which followed the rest of the building in still having its original features and equipment.

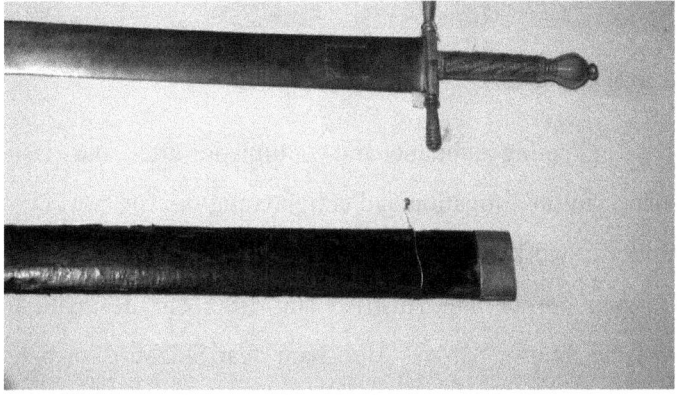

(The Judgement sword; either you were hung or pulled apart by wild horses)

When we were introduced to Theresita she explained that the castle was open to the public as a museum, and that she also conducted tours of the castle for children, where they got to learn about the history attached to the building. I was fascinated to learn that the castle actually dated back as far as 1191, and was named after the Moosheimer people who were the first family it belonged to. The castle itself was largely built out of

Roman stones which were taken from a nearby village. As if all of this wasn't impressive enough, Theresita also told us that the Castle actually had three courtyards. No matter where you turned in this huge place, there were always new surprises or interesting pieces of history to uncover.

I found that I instantly liked Austria. I loved not only the Castle before us, but also the breath-taking Austrian landscape and countryside that surrounded us. I also sympathised with Theresita, as she explained to us some of the activity that was reported there and confided that she hated going into the castle, especially after dark, as she had also had quite a few paranormal experiences herself. I hoped that we could try and bring some reassurance to her through our investigation here.

Patrick and Theresita's interview went extremely well. Immediately before even crossing the drawbridge, Patrick picked up on children, but more importantly for Theresita, Patrick picked up that although a huge amount of horrible things had happened here, there were also light aspects to it. For example, in one of the castle courtyards Patrick sensed animals and also some people who had at one time or other lived here. These particular spirits he explained, were returning not because they were trapped, or because of anything horrible, but simply because they loved the place while they were alive. They were just visiting. You could evidently see Theresita's relief that not everything in this Castle was scary and as the interview and Patrick's walk around progressed, she slowly became more comfortable.

I have gone into some detail on this because it is important to understand that our work is not just for the sake of our filming, nor yet for the spirits we help and sometimes rescue, but also for the people who are still living or working in these places. When you're a paranormal investigator, the work encapsulates everything and everybody involved, and a lot of times we arrive to find that some or all of the people currently living or working in these places are themselves anxious or fearful of the activity that occurs. Hence, it is then our job to try and give them some reassurance and help them.

While Patrick continued his walk around and interview with Theresita, it again left some time for Jamie, Ben and I to explore our surroundings. During our visit we were staying in the cabins used as accommodation for guests there, which for us was brilliant. Each of the cabins was set out with all of the amenities of a 'miniature flat', including a separate bathroom and kitchen. In addition to the cabins, the grounds themselves were surrounded by beautiful woodland. While we explored the area we came across a woodland path, which led up into the trees. As we followed the path, we climbed higher and higher into the trees, enjoying the myriad of different trees and shrubs which bordered each side of the dirt path, the wild flowers that were growing there, listening to the soothing sounds of the birds and hearing rustling as one small animal or another scuttled through the bordering undergrowth. It was magical. Once we reached the highest point of the hill, we were in for another surprise as we turned and looked at the view. You could see the landscape for miles, not to mention a great view of the castle building itself. For a good few hours we enjoyed this stunning woodland walk before heading back to meet with the others.

(The forest surrounding the castle)

Later that day Patrick and Karl briefed us on just what they had found during the rest of the walk around with Theresita, and it only served to make us more eager to investigate the Castle further. Every inch of the building had an interesting story to tell. In one of the main large halls for example, there was a huge wooden beam which stretched from one end of the hall to the other. Theresita informed us that this beam was actually made from one entire trunk of a tree. Other impressive items included a display of guns, which we later learned were the guns of illegal poachers who had been caught. In the past, if a hunter was found guilty of poaching he was shot with his own gun, and what we were seeing displayed on the walls was the collection of guns confiscated from many of the poachers who had been caught. Another interesting artefact was a magnificent horse drawn coach – which again we were informed was actually used by archduchess Marie Theresa, the only female ruler of Habsburg empire which included Austria and Hungary.

("Some" of the many poachers guns on display)

If somebody had told me that we would be investigating a castle that not only has a lot of history in itself, but is also a museum, which housed the coach used by Marie Theresa who ruled half of Europe at the time, not to mention a glorious wealth of other priceless and timeless items, I would have thought them mad. I felt privileged to be there. We even had a brief glance at the torture rooms, where a lot of the original furniture and equipment had been preserved. Ben, Jamie and I sat listening to Patrick and Karl relaying all of this with rapt attention, and I couldn't help growing more excited at the prospect of investigating further and holding the physical circle that evening.

(Queen Marie Theresa's Coach)

We headed back to the rooms we were staying in to rest and have something to eat before our big investigation that evening. I always find it curious how wherever we stay, the rooms we stay in (even if in a separate hotel), are often just as haunted as the main place we are filming in. The rooms we stayed in while filming at Moosham were no exception. A lot of the Ghostcircle team heard unexplained footsteps or saw shadows in our rooms, and Patrick told us he was also picking up on a spirit who haunted the place. When we spoke to Theresita, she also told us that people had also been surprised to learn when she had been away on holiday, as they reported hearing footsteps and noises in the cabins. Naturally, assuming it was Theresita walking around, it somewhat surprised them when they realised she had in fact been away at that time.

    Once we had all the cameras set up and ready, we headed back over to the main castle building. The huge castle looked far more imposing and intimidating at night, with just the moonlight to cast an eerie glow over the ancient stonework. It's difficult, although irrational, not to suddenly call to mind every horror movie you've ever watched as you look at such a sight, and despite our excitement, we huddled close together as we made our way over the drawbridge, watching our step so as not to get our feet caught in the gaps between the wooden slats. As we reached the main entrance door, Patrick stopped, turned toward us, and warned that we should all keep hold of the hand of the person in front of us for safety, so as not to get lost. The hairs rose on the back of my neck as myself, Jamie and Ben looked at each other, and with that caution in mind, we headed into the castle to uncover the dark secrets within.

(Night time at Schloss Moosham)

It soon became very apparent why Patrick had cautioned us to keep close together. In the pitch black you could only see a couple of feet, if that, in front of you. We walked up narrow staircases and along large corridors where you could see numerous doors on each side. It was easy to see that if you inadvertently walked through the wrong door or took a wrong turn, you could become lost very easily in the vast maze of rooms. On we went, ascending yet more stairs and climbing higher into the castle. Eventually, we came to a large hall, which had a smaller room to the back. There was a perfect table for us to use for the circle, there were chairs in one corner of the room, and in the smaller room at the back there was even an old wooden baby's cradle, which we were to find would be important later.

As we settled down ready to start the circle I felt excited and also was wondering how Theresita would find it. It was clear to us that she was also very intuitive, and earlier had shared with us some of the experiences she had had and the things she had sensed. However, Theresita was also quite nervous of the castle and confided that she never entered the castle alone at night, which was very understandable given some of the dark history and the vast size of the building.

The circle actually turned out to be extremely interesting. After Patrick had helped to build up the energy, he asked Theresita to go over to stand with him, and she could actually see the transfiguration that was taking place, and saw her grandfather's face appearing and taking shape over Patrick's face. It was great to see her reaction to what was happening and to see her relaxing a bit more and feeling more at ease as time went on. I mentioned transfiguration just now, and some people may be wondering what that is and how it happens.

Transfiguration in essence is, when a spirit uses the medium's energy to try and manifest so that other people present may see them. Usually this means that their image will appear and take form over the medium's own features which can often appear to look a bit like a hologram. As the spirit is first trying to manifest it can sometimes look quite frightening especially if you have never experienced it. The medium's face appears to shift and change, and the features often become distorted or even disappear altogether. Patrick often explains that the reason for this is because as strange as it may sound, the spirit is trying to 'remember' what they looked like in life and trying to replicate this. Remember that when a person dies, they no longer have a physical body. Added to that the fact they may have died many years before, and, although it's not in the context of this book to explain this in detail, may have had many other previous lives on earth, it can then be understandable to see why it can be difficult to remember exactly what you looked like!

It then came time for Ben, Jamie, and I to do our ghost hunt. The energy in the room was definitely palpable. You could see the blue mist enveloping everything in the room, and the rods stretching between our fingers when we held our hands out towards each other. As the three of us started to walk around the room, I felt confident that we would pick something up and even catch some good EVP's on our voice recorder.

Jamie said that he could sense a man walking around the room towards the back where there was a small side room, that appeared to have been used as a nursery at one time, and so this is where we headed. As we approached our destination, I could feel the energy becoming denser and heavier. Suddenly, all three of us stopped where we were and stared at each other. We soon realised from the confused looks we exchanged that none of us had caused the vibration we felt through the floor. Footsteps!

I asked the question out loud if they had felt the footsteps. Jamie and Ben confirmed that they had felt it too. Although we are investigating the paranormal, we also exercise common sense when interpreting things that happen so every logical reason for something naturally occurring is checked out first. This is perhaps one of the most important aspects of paranormal investigation. It is very easy to get carried away in the moment and mistake simple occurrences – a net curtain moving due to a breeze from an open window (just as an example) – for paranormal phenomena. Therefore usually when something happens, we look around and examine our surroundings for anything that potentially may have caused it, and in some cases also ask the spirit to repeat what they did in order to confirm it was paranormal.

In this particular case in order to confirm that the ghostly footsteps were genuine paranormal phenomena, we all made sure to stand very still and listened. Sure enough we heard the footsteps again. My excitement instantly rose and we began to ask questions to see if we could get any communication from whoever was there. We quite often find that the energy rarely stays still. Instead, it is more fluid and moves from place to place. It was the same in this case too. It seemed to move further into the small back room where the wooden cradle was, and so we followed it.

I could feel that the energy had become much denser now, and we could still hear the footsteps and various taps around us. We continued asking questions to see what EVP's we could find when going through the footage later. At one point I realised I had one hand on the cradle. Ben was standing next to me. Without warning, we felt a sharp tap on the crib, as if somebody had banged on it with their hand. Neither myself nor Ben had moved, while Jamie had also seen that neither of us had moved at all and yet, both myself and Ben had felt the tap.

We then moved back into the main hall where we continued to get responses to the questions we asked. At one point the spirit of the man that seemed to be haunting the room even physically pushed me. It was certainly a shock as I had never experienced that before, but we soon made a joke of it by Patrick asking if the Spirit could answer by giving "one push for yes, two for no!" I was enjoying this investigation and we seemed to be getting a lot of phenomena. However, before long it was time to close the circle and bring the investigation to an end. As we always do, we thanked Spirit for their help and closed the circle. Patrick also said a prayer to help the Spirit that was still present there to move on and we had a lovely message from the spirits, when the K2 meter started to light up just as we asked for a release. Theresita who was sitting with us also gave some clairvoyance and she also picked up information from the Spirits herself, as she is also a very sensitive soul and it was truly amazing to watch.

I think it's safe to say that Moosham Castle had exceeded all of our expectations. It's sheer size alone, combined with the beautiful Austrian landscape surrounding it made it an impressive building, and as we piled back into the car to leave, I felt confident that we had managed to capture some great phenomena on camera and looked forward to watching the final edited footage. On our investigation of Moosham Castle ending, another door opened on our next one, and I looked forward to the adventures it would bring.

Malaspina Castle

(Looking over the village roofs from a window in Malaspina Castle)

For our next filming trip, we headed across the border to Italy. Our destination this time was the beautiful mountain town of Fosdinovo located in Tuscany, to investigate "Castello Malaspina di Fosdinovo", or Malaspina Castle.

I remember as we were driving along marvelling at the beautiful Italian hills we were driving through. It was unlike any country I had seen before, with wonderful quaint villages at the base of the hills, as well as picturesque houses actually built into the side of the hills. The houses from a distance looked stunningly beautiful, while also seeming that they may fall from where they perched at any second. As we made our way up the winding roads, I noticed also that every so often the ground levelled off a bit and there would be a side or slip road that led to other small villages dotted around the hilly landscape, that were not immediately evident from lower down the hills.

As we climbed higher into the hills the road gradually gave way to soil and the smooth motion of the car gradually became increasingly bumpier. The twists and turns in the road became increasingly more difficult to negotiate. I soon realised we were travelling along what must have been an old goat track. A glance outside of the right hand side window showed a spectacular view, as well as a treacherously steep drop. As careful a driver as Karl is, the car was barely wide enough to fit on the road safely, and as we made jokes to lighten the mood we prayed we would get to the top of the hill and onto wider and safer ground before we met any oncoming cars (as unbelievable as it may seem, this narrow road was in fact the main route up and down the hill). The fact was, that our SatNav took us on the "shortest route" to the castle, probably knocking off a minute of time. It was not exactly the safest route up to the castle, and as the wheels of our SUV were just wide enough to go up the goat track, we had a very steep bank looming down my side of the window out of which, Ben, Jamie and I looked down the cliff side very nervously as the wheels literally edged along. Of course when we left the castle afterwards, we saw there was a perfectly fine "A" road to take us safely down the mountain – I couldn't believe it! Although in hindsight we could also see the humour of the situation.

Eventually we reached the top of the hill and sighed in relief that we had arrived in one piece. The next shock came when we looked at the building itself. The entrance hall in itself was enormous, with massive old heavy wooden doors that gave you a slight sense that you were entering Dracula's lair as you walked through. The thick stone walls and long main staircase with its wide and uneven stone steps showed the castle's impressive age, and I was intrigued to learn more of the building's history and haunted tales.

(The front door and stairs leading up to the castle courtyard)

The lady that met us as we arrived introduced herself and she would do some of the Italian / English interpretation with some of the staff before leading us around on a grand tour of the castle. The castle had the obligatory front castle courtyard and there was also an inner courtyard rectangular in shape and surrounded on all four sides by the imposing darkened castle walls. The main hall was enormous, and it felt as if it took an age to walk from one end of this great room to another. As might be expected in a castle, there were also a number of towers (one of which Ben would have the unenvied privilege of sleeping in alone – little did he know).

Malaspina Castle has very famous connection with Dante Alighieri who actually lived here for a few months when he was in exile. The castle still has his bed in the room where he wrote some of his famous writings. After the tour of the castle, we were shown up to the rooms where we would be staying. As we came to the base of the stairs to one of the tower rooms, Ben looked at the lady showing us around.

"Who's going to be up there?" he asked. Considering Patrick, Karl and Jamie and I had already been shown our rooms, the answer was obvious. When the penny dropped, the nervous look on his face was amusing to watch, although the truth be told it could have made even the devil himself nervous sleeping in one of those tower rooms alone.

(Patrick at Dante's desk with his bust on top of it)

As we started to prepare for that evening's filming, I took a quick look around the area we were filming in the castle. For some reason the atmosphere in the building felt more oppressive than the other places. Whether it was in part simply due to the size of the place, I'm not sure, but there seemed to be a slightly more sinister feeling in the air that instinctively caused you to keep your guard up. When I voiced this to the others, they also agreed.

By now, everything was ready and so we started to open our psychic senses to see what we could pick up on. Almost instantly Patrick was drawn to the inner courtyard. Indeed, there was a lot of energy present there, and we all kept seeing shadows darting across out of the corners of our eyes. Our voice recorders at the ready, we asked questions and tried to see if we could communicate with them. After a few minutes of this, we decided to split up in order to try and cover more ground, and so, armed with an infra-red camera, Jamie, Ben and I set off to investigate the lower halls of the building as this was another area that we had identified as being quite 'active'.

All three of us entered the lower main hall, almost in military formation, each of us doing our best to keep a 360 degree view of what was around us, in case anything should suddenly jump out. The room itself was vast. It was a fair width and very long, with lovely pictures adorning the walls and a few benches scattered along the edge of the room. We made our way cautiously to a bench along the wall at one end of the room. We at least felt a little more secure with our backs against the wall, although with the room being so long and in complete darkness, it was difficult to see all the way to the far end of the hall.

(Patrick admiring the wall fresco in the great hall)

After sitting there for a couple of minutes, Ben suddenly exclaimed that he could see something at the far end of the hall. We looked in the direction he indicated and sure enough we could see a mass of energy there. It's difficult to describe as it was unlike anything any of us had seen before. This mass of white energy seemed alive and we watched in astonishment as it twisted and turned and rolled along the floor at the far end of the room. To this day I'm still not completely sure of what it was we were seeing that night, but what I can say is none of us were willing to walk to the far end of the room alone to investigate! This was something we could not explain and it unnerved us a little, but we carried on with the investigation.

(Ben and Jamie in the castle dungeon during the investigation)

We did spend some time asking questions hoping that we may then get a response from this entity that seemed to be present. Of course, throughout our filming, each of us take our roles in the group and the filming work very seriously; we do like to have a joke every now and then just to lighten the mood. As we walked back down the hall we heard a whisper. I wasn't able to make out what it said but as one, Jamie, Ben and I immediately halted in our tracks.

"Did you hear that!?" I whispered to Jamie. He nodded, and Ben confirmed he had heard it too. Then we heard it again. Now we all huddled closer, almost afraid to find out what was making the sound, until Karl turned on his flashlight and suddenly came into view, sitting a little way off from us with a big grin on his face. Relief flooded over me as we laughed it off and I did my best to sound stern as I scolded Karl for playing such a prank on us!

After the excitement of our investigation, and with the night wearing on, we decided eventually that it was best to turn in for the night. Again, Ben understandably glanced nervously at the lonely tower steps leading to the room in the top of the turret. Jamie and I were in the room directly below, so we did our best to reassure him that he could call us or stay in our room if it became too much for him sleeping there. Patrick also reiterated the same thing, but to each of us Ben declined.

Jamie and I settled in for the night. Well, when I say "settled in", I mean that I was lying on my back as stiff as a board and terrified to move. Something in the room did not feel right. It almost felt as if the room was divided in two. One half of the room felt lighter, the air less dense, whereas the second half of the room (where I was), seemed to have a decidedly more sinister feeling. The air felt heavier as if it was pressing in on you. I thought Jamie was asleep beside me, but suddenly he lifted his head slightly. "Do you see that?"

"What?" I said. He pointed to the left hand side of the room, and when I looked, indeed I could see what he was talking about. The white, twisting, turning energy we had seen in the lower halls during our investigation was there. I confirmed that I could see it, and both of us just looked at each other and made an unspoken agreement not to move from the bed!

I then saw a white figure move from the en-suite bathroom across the bedroom to the desk that was in the middle of the room, before suddenly vanishing. I couldn't believe it. I could not make out any features, but the figure was completely solid. The image was like a perfectly white silhouette of a person that looked as if a life size model had been cut from white card. It was the most solid that I have seen a spirit so far. Jamie had seen my reaction, and I told him what I had seen.

"Oh my God!" he exclaimed. "What!?" I was wide-eyed with panic at what I was about to hear. "Well, I didn't like to say..." he continued, "but just before you said that I heard water running in the bathroom – it sounded as if the taps were being turned on and off."

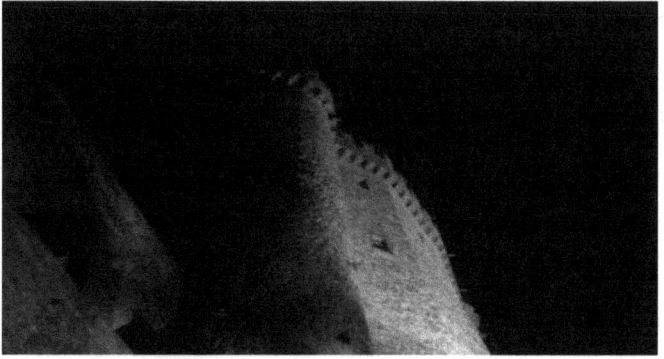
(The outside of the castle tower at night)

Needless to say, both of us found it difficult after that to get to sleep. We sat up staring around the room to see if we could see anything else. I could sense a presence on the right hand side of the room and a few minutes later I felt a pressure on top of the bed, just as if somebody had sat on the edge of the bed and was leaning over. Jamie was lying on my other side, so I knew it couldn't be him. I told him what was happening and seeing the worry on my face, he asked if I wanted to swap sides so he was lying on my side of the bed. I declined. I didn't see any point in that as we were still experiencing paranormal activity regardless of where we were in the room. Eventually, the activity settled down enough that we could finally settle down to sleep. To this day I have to admit that is probably one of the only places I have stayed in that have truly frightened me to the point where I almost wanted to run out there and then.

(One of the grand bedrooms in the castle)

The following morning at breakfast, we were eager to recount our experiences of the previous night. "So did you experience anything last night? Did you film anything in your rooms?"

Jamie and I looked at each other before telling of everything that had happened the night before. We also confirmed that we had used the camera to film some of our experiences, although how well it had come out we didn't know. Ben had not said anything to any of us about his night and he remained quiet. So we both thought that perhaps that nothing had really happened in his room that night. However, he surprised all of us by saying that he had in fact encountered a Spirit who kept poking him in the side. He was so terrified that he slept with the light on and did not even move from the bed to go to the bathroom. As amusing as a spirit playfully poking him in the side sounded, he was clearly terrified by the experience. "Why didn't you call one of us?" we said, "or come down to our room?" His answer was simple:

"I was too scared! I didn't want to move from where I was!"

"But why didn't you call one of us then, on your phone?"

"I didn't want to", Ben replied. It may seem like quite a paradox, but I consider Ben to possibly be the most courageous out of all of us. To stick something out when you are not scared is easy, especially when you are with somebody else, but to stick it out when you're on your own and terrified takes real courage. It may have purely been stubbornness, but I admired him for sticking it through nonetheless, especially as he still kept coming along with us to other investigations despite any previous scary experiences.

And so our adventure at the atmospheric Malaspina Castle ended. As we left I thought over everything that we had experienced. It had definitely been one of the most active places I had been to, in terms of paranormal activity. I was sure that we had caught some EVP's on the recorders as well as plenty of activity on the cameras. Later on we played back the audio and you can clearly hear the word "Dante" during a question and answer session in his room at the castle. There some amazing EVP's which you can hear on this episode. It had been an amazing experience, and one I was immensely glad of having had the opportunity to be a part of.

(Castle Malaspina di Fosdinovo)

Suasmarez Manor

(Patrick with Peter de Sausmarez in the manor hallway)

One of the most captivating places we have investigated, for me personally, was Sausmarez Manor which is in Guernsey. The Manor itself had an air of peace and serenity about it. To get there you had to get to the top of steep hill which leads out from the capital, St Peter Port. Once you arrived there, you had what felt like a mile trek up the long, winding gravel drive before you reached the house. It was a magnificent and beautiful place. And when I say 'house', that is a massive understatement, as it was in fact a beautiful Manor. Extending out from the impressive main building, were grounds and gardens that seemed to go on for acres. When you were walking around the grounds, it really almost felt like an entire village in itself – each corner you turned revealed something new, a different wonderful surprise that added to the whole ambience of the grounds and building.

We pulled up outside the main building, and Peter Sausmarez greeted us warmly. I liked him instantly. He was a very charismatic character. He started telling us about the manor, and naturally our conversation led on to talking about the Paranormal. When we eventually asked if there were any intriguing stories, and paranormal activity that had taken place, his eyes lit up.

"Oh yes!" he replied, and then went on to explain how he offers haunted tours to the public, where he escorts them around the beautiful manor and tells them stories about the different ghosts that are there, and all the experiences that both he and other people have had in the Manor. He had a way of making the stories come to life, and he told them with such enthusiasm that it was impossible not to get drawn into what he was saying.

Peter de Sausmarez has a title of Lord, or Seigneur in French, from where the original title originates. The family are steeped in history with the family name going back to 1117. They have been with Kings and Queens, have historic military and naval connections. His ancestors took a ship full of Spanish gold one of the biggest seizures in history, out of which the family used to rebuild the manor house. Another famous Admiral de Sausmarez fought with Nelson, and even Peter himself has been on guard for the Queen at Buckingham Palace. He also led the trooping the colours on her birthday, which is quite a significant honour, and there is a wonderful silver statue in the house which was presented to him by his colleagues afterwards. Sir Edmund Andros, was in 1674 both Bailiff and Lieutenant Governor of Guernsey and at the same time Governor of the Colony of New York as well as New England, North Carolina, Virginia, Massachusetts, New Plymouth and New Jersey. In fact it was he, who changed the name from New Amsterdam to New York, when he was its first British Governor.

(Statue presented to Peter de Sausmarez by his colleagues)

Once initial introductions were over, we were shown up to the rooms where we would be staying. My first impression as we were led up the grand staircase was just complete admiration. I was in awe of the buildings and the beautiful grounds, as well as the effort that the family had put into it. My only concern was really how on earth we were going to find our way in this place! It was such a large building with a warren of different corridors, halls, rooms and doors that I knew it was going to take a good while for me to learn my way around.

I was also amazed when we went into the room where we would be staying. Well, at least we expected it to be a room. Instead, we found to our delight in that it was actually much more of a small flat on the top floor of the Manor. Jamie and I were thrilled, and we couldn't wait to start unpacking our things and enjoy the few days that we were going to be there.

Our next port of call, as we had a little extra time to play with before starting filming, was to explore the wonderful grounds surrounding the property. I found one of my favourite parts of the grounds tucked away to the left side of the property. Patrick first alerted me to it as we made our way back to the car. He knew it was something that I would be interested in, and once he led me there, I could see why. I love animals and work in a veterinary surgery, and so it comes as no surprise that I also love horses, and horse riding.

At the back of the house there was what used to be horse stables. In the middle of the courtyard there was a big well, which used to be where the horses could drink. Patrick explained that they would have bred and raised working and competition horses here. As I walked around the old stables, I could almost visualise the horses that would have been here, the activity there would have been in the courtyard as they trained and cared for the horses, and it was amazing to be able to see where they would have been kept. After visiting the stables, we packed into the car and headed off to buy food and snacks for our room, and by the time we got back it was time to start our filming.

I knew that myself, Jamie and Ben would be doing our part of the investigation later in the evening… and for this reason, as a rule of thumb I usually don't like to know anything about what Patrick may have picked up on his walk-around – in case it affects our investigation later. However, I was intrigued, partly because of the grand buildings, and partly because of what Peter Sausmarez had already told us; as to what kinds of paranormal stories and ghosts would reveal themselves here. So I decided on this occasion that I would actually like to see what Patrick would find on his tour with Peter. In fact, more than that as we walked around I made an effort to try and see what, if anything, I was picking up on myself. Admittedly, my mediumistic abilities were nowhere close to Patrick's level of psychic perception, but I found that I could pick up on the energies that were around – and for the most part, what I sensed was there correlated with what Patrick was saying, the difference being that Patrick then added more detail to the information I was getting.

One of my favourite rooms in the Manor was the gorgeous dining room. Furnished with a long banquet table and beautiful chairs, lavishly decorated with family portraits on the walls opposite which there were elegant windows letting in bright sunlight. It was very picturesque. Patrick then said he could sense the presence of a man there, standing by a door that communicated with the hall and adjoining room. To our surprise, Peter then confirmed that indeed there *was* a presence in that room, and not only that, but that the door where we had sensed this presence frequently opened on its own accord. There were also plenty of other ghost tales and experiences as we made our way from room to room in the Manor, one being about a story of the ghost of a kindly lady who, coincidentally in a separate building where we were staying during our trip, liked to look out for and keep an eye on children that were there. Now, it's not always conducive to a good night's sleep knowing there's a ghost around… but we felt relieved that at least the ghosts in this Manor appeared to be friendly!

On this particular trip, we also had our friend Tracy Edwards come along with us. She is a fantastic medium, and also practices trance mediumship, as well as clairvoyance and being a gifted Reiki master. So before we went ahead with our investigation, we sat in circle that evening with Peter de Sausmarez and his friends, and Tracy kindly agreed to allow a spirit (who coincidentally also goes by the name of Peter!) to work through her. Peter is a kindly soul who often works with and communicates through Tracy when she goes into trance. The information that is provided is not just practical information, but it also personal information and advice, which normally relates to what is happening in a person's life at that very moment. Having had some communications myself, I can say it is amazingly accurate.

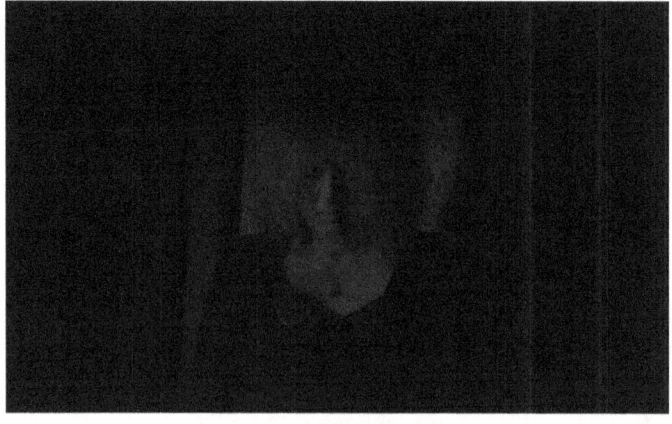

(Tracy Edwards in Trance with her guide 'Peter' speaking through her)

There is a lot of scepticism that can surround trance mediumship, and I must admit that when I first met Tracy, I did wonder myself whether it was truly trance or simply an "act" being put on. I remember the first time that I saw Tracy go into trance, I was listening to Peter speak and scrutinizing everything that was happening – the tone of voice, Tracy's body language and movements, as well as what was being said. However, no matter how hard I might have tried, I could not come to any other conclusion other than what I was seeing, was indeed very real. Her voice goes deeper, too deep for a person to be able to consciously change their voice to that degree – and the level of insight and information that is given you can tell goes beyond what Tracy herself would know sometimes. It's difficult to explain in the confines of the pages of a book, I think really you have to experience it for yourself to decide, and approach it with an open mind – but certainly from my own experience in observing her trance – both Tracy and Peter certainly made a believer out of me!

As we set up the circle and took our places, I wondered how the people here would react. Most of them had never seen trance before, and I hoped that they would approach the experience with an open mind.

Tracy relaxed down and went into a meditation to blend with the spirit of Peter. There was an air of anticipation in the room as we waited, and after a few minutes, I heard Peter's familiar and strong voice greet the group. After initially explaining to everyone who he was, he then opened it up to the floor and asked if anybody wanted to ask a question.

What happened next proved to be very interesting. It was well known within the Sausmarez family that during the war some treasure had been hidden by Peter's cousin Cecil somewhere in the vast grounds surrounding the manor. This was done in order to prevent it being seized and taken into the wrong hands. For a long time, they had been trying unsuccessfully to recover this treasure, so therefore this is what their question revolved around – where in the grounds had the treasure been buried. I could feel the level of expectation in the room, and this, coupled with the fact that Tracy was working in an unfamiliar environment and also had never been filmed during trance before, made it more difficult to work easily.

However, Peter came through Tracy and conveyed lots of information to them. He did in fact tell them the answer to their question and that they would find it. It is also worth pointing out here, that when Spirit gives us answers to our questions, it is not always completely straightforward and they do not always just hand the answer to us on a plate – after all, we need to make some effort for ourselves too! Peter did however describe the location in the grounds where they would find the treasure. I think, maybe because Peter's answer had not come in the way that the group had expected with an X marks the spot answer, that they seemed confused and frustrated at first. However, Patrick stepped in briefly and helped to clarify some details, rephrasing and explaining what Peter had said, until eventually they understood. If I had not had a hundred per cent conviction in my belief of the Spirit world before, then I certainly did now! It was almost too amazing to put into words. Here we were, in a strange place where we had never been, with unfamiliar people we had never met before, and yet the spirit of Peter had just told them exactly where to find this family treasure that they had been unsuccessful in recovering for years. I also greatly admired Tracy's ability as a medium – it's not every person that would be able to go into trance in that way and get such fantastic results!

Once Tracy had completed her trance, it was then time for us to begin our own investigation and see if we could pick up on any of the spirits that Patrick had picked up on earlier or if we could pick up any EVP's. I always find it intriguing how on some occasions we tend to pick up on information really easily, and yet other times you really have to work to be able to find anything at all. On this occasion, it seemed all three of us were having a bit of difficulty at pinning anything down for very long. It was like we were 'chasing' the energy around the room. I could sense that something was there and could feel the tangible energy, but it was almost like trying to grab hold of mist at times – and then once we did start communicating with a spirit, after a short while the energy appeared to fade and go 'dead', and move on, and we would have to find it again.

When this sort of chasing the energy happens, it can be for a number of different reasons. Sometimes it may be that a spirit is shy or wary of communicating, and other times it can be simply because the conditions are just not quite right to allow the spirit to communicate (for example if somebody is fearful). In any case, it can make it much more challenging to pick up on information and relay the stories of the Spirits we encounter, but it also adds excitement and variety – you just never know what you are going to get, and that's part of what I love about being in Ghostcircle.

Despite this slight frustration, it was an amazing place to work and we did pick up some amazing EVP's and phenomena there. I find it most humbling when the people or spirits that we pick up on hold a message or some other significance for the people who we are working with. Quite often, especially if people have had unexplained experiences, it can be a great relief and bring a sense of closure for them having their experiences validated by the information that we pick up. It also helps the Spirits that we work with. It has been my experience so far, that a lot of the time these souls simply want their stories to be shared and heard by others. Perhaps that's because when they were alive, there may have been certain societal restrictions within the communities or time period they were living in that meant they were unable to speak out then. But they still have a desire and the opportunity for their story to be heard now. Of course, there are also those spirits that simply visit from time to time because they loved the place when they were alive. Additionally, there are spirits who may even have a connection with somebody living there today. Either way, I feel it allows closure and a sense of peace for both the Spirit and the people who are living there, which for me, gives meaning to the work that we do.

In this case, Peter de Sausmarez already appeared at ease with the spiritual world and you can see that this is evident in the haunted tours that he offered, combined with his enthusiasm when talking about his experiences and the spirits that reside there. This helped to make it a lot easier for us to communicate with the spirits there and to pick up on the energies in each room. The exquisite Manor had its own unique stories and character, as does each venue we visit, and that in itself makes the place come alive with its own, unique energy.

That night, when we went back to the small flat we were staying in, we took one of the smaller cameras with us and decided we would film and try and see if we could catch any paranormal activity happening overnight. It has been reported, that there was the spirit of a kindly nanny, who used to help look after the children when she was alive, and she was said to haunt this part of the Manor. In the past there had been a number of sightings reported of her. We wanted to see if we could communicate with her or any of the other spirits that may be there.

Although we had only been there a short while, both Jamie and myself had felt a strong energy there and seen shapes moving out of the corner of our eye. That night, as we sat there in the bedroom, we saw quite clearly of what appeared to be the figure of a lady walk right past the bedroom door down the hall. We both looked at each other, and could tell from each other's reactions that we had both seen her.

We grabbed the camera and the voice recorder, and followed where we thought the lady had gone, into the living area of the flat. What I found there, however, was not what I had expected. Instead of seeing the spirit of the lady, I could instead sense the spirit of a young boy. It was almost like watching a child playing, and I could sense his presence behind one of the chairs. There was clearly more than just one spirit haunting this place.

I asked Jamie if he could see the little boy, to which he replied he could not, but he was able to sense the energy there. I looked around the room, although I could now no longer see or sense the spirit of the lady we had seen. I felt that she, like a lot of the spirits here, was a visiting spirit, and that she simply came once in a while to visit a place that she clearly loved and felt a strong connection to in life. Turning my attention back to the boy, I walked over to where I could sense him. I could see the familiar, blue, translucent energy that I often saw when we conduct our investigations, and when I placed my hand into this energy, I could feel the tingling sensation of it against my skin. Jamie did the same and voiced what he was able to see and feel too.

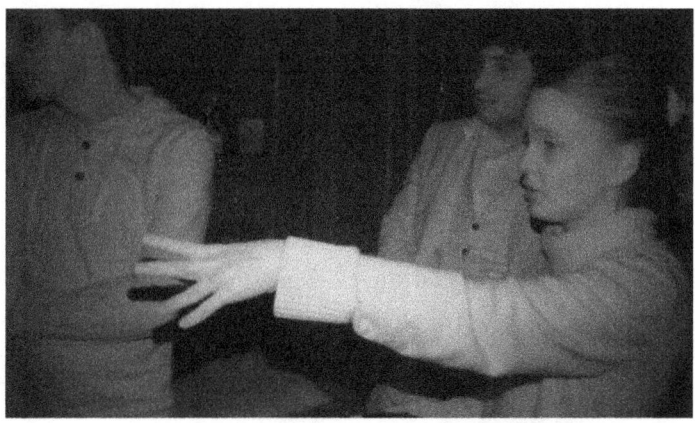

("Me" directing the boys, during the Ghost Hunt)

I was feeling quite excited about this. Apart from our investigation at Malaspina Castle, this was the first place where I had really sensed anything significant in the room where we were staying. I found that amazing. And, as always I also felt humbled by the fact that we were able to communicate with the spirits here, and listen to their stories. I always find that if you treat them with respect (for they are people too), they are the souls of people who have lived lives on earth the same as us and deserve the same level of courtesy and respect. If you take this approach, then the majority of the time they are amenable and willing to have their unique stories told. So we sat for a few minutes talking to this little boy and asking questions, and we still had the voice recorder with us to see if we could pick up any EVP's too.

We picked up on a couple more pieces of information, but then had to call it a night. Both of us were starting to feel tired and drained. Whenever we do spiritual work, it can in some cases be very taxing, as it not only tires us physically, but it also depletes our energy because Spirit need to use this in order to be able to manifest and communicate with us here on the physical earth plane. This is also one of the reasons it is important to be careful with ensuring that you 'close down' properly after working, as otherwise your energy can continue to be depleted. By doing this as well it helps in protecting you from any other lower energies that may try and feed off your energy.

The following morning when we met up again with the team, we were excited to tell them what we picked up on and had experienced the previous night. We felt confident that we had caught a lot of EVP's on the voice recorder, as well as some evidence on film. Along with Tracy's trance demonstration, I knew that this would certainly make for an interesting episode in the Ghostcircle series we were filming.

Although we all work hard on the filming on these trips, we also like to take some time out, as mentioned before, to enjoy and explore the different places and areas that we visit. On this occasion, myself and Jamie really wanted to explore the vast grounds that housed this beautiful manor. The grounds of Sausmarez Manor are actually opened to the public, and during the day there is a vast array of different activities for people to do and places to explore, catering for all different ages to make it family friendly. As we walked around, we saw different stalls set up in a kind of marketplace, selling many wonderfully intriguing paintings and various other items. There was also a copper workshop, where different ornaments and statues were hand crafted for people to buy. I ended up purchasing a beautiful ornament from there of a horse and foal, which I loved.

There was also a woodland trail which I felt excited to explore. I love spending time in woodland and surrounded by nature, and so, walking along this nature trail seemed the perfect thing for us to do. The sun was shining, which made the walk even more pleasant and the light from the sun enhanced the beauty of everything around us. I enjoy spending time in nature because if I sit or stand quietly for a moment, I can feel the energy that encompasses and pulses through every living thing. It's almost like a gentle hum that you can feel coming from the earth itself and imbuing everything with life. I do believe that everyone can sense this energy to one degree or another. Think of when you walk through woodland, or a field, or anywhere where you are surrounded by nothing except nature. Think of how peaceful it feels and how refreshed you can sometimes feel after spending some time in such a place. This is the same kind of energy that I'm talking about here. It may not be anything completely out of this world, but it is a powerful energy and feeling nonetheless. It was a beautiful trail walk that we were on, and it made me appreciate the grounds and this place even more as we walked around. When it finally came time to leave this remarkable place, I felt very grateful that we had come here and had been welcomed by Peter de

Sausmarez and his family to film here. It was exciting to think of what the next adventure would bring.

Clonony Castle

(Clonony Castle on a beautiful summer's day)

Our travels then took us across to Ireland, where we had the opportunity to film at the renowned Clonony Castle owned by Rebecca Black. Ireland in itself has a unique energy of its own, completely and totally different from anywhere else I have been so far. I had a sense that this had something to do with the sheer amount of greenery and fields and farms in this characteristic country. Ben, Jamie and the other members of our team could also feel it. We could all sense the wonderful energy that surrounded us, and Patrick mentioned that there were actually quite a lot of nature spirits in Ireland.

As we approached Clonony Castle, my first impression was that it appeared very imposing. I remember as we parked up and got out of the car, we were nearly bowled over by a huge gust of wind – which somehow only seemed to add to the impressive atmosphere of the building. As we arrived, Rebecca Black came out to greet us. She was a lovely lady – very eccentric and fun to be around.

We spent a while talking generally about the castle and its history, to which I was extremely surprised and amazed to learn that the Boleyn sisters of Anne Boleyn and Henry VIII fame, had once lived here. While we were outside, Patrick had picked up on a lady who he felt was important and had died here. When he relayed this to Rebecca, she told us that the Boleyn sisters had actually been here and one of them had jumped from the roof to her death. It was an exciting piece of history to discover, and I couldn't wait to investigate and find out more.

I could tell that the castle itself was very old. One of the things that struck me most, was that outside, there were some very steep steps on the outside of the building, but once you got into the castle, the steps, although still inclining at quite a steep angle, were much narrower and uneven. It added a great deal to the authenticity and character of the castle, although it also meant you had to watch your step when climbing the stairs up to the tower. I liked Rebecca Black as she had great energy and enthusiasm. It was really great watching Patrick interact with her and explaining what he was picking up with her as we did the initial walk around the place. He gave Rebecca a reading too, after which she confirmed was quite accurate. I think when Patrick does a reading, it can sometimes help the connection to Spirit for the rest of the investigation, as it helps to build a rapport between the person hosting us and the team.

Patrick picked up some amazing things on his walk around, and it was clear that there were again some very interesting (and prominent!) spirits here. The main challenge for us on this particular trip was the weather! There was an Atlantic storm coming in with a fierce wind when we arrived that had not let up, so we could hear the howling noise it made outside and we did our best to persevere with the filming while working around it. Strangely, or perhaps not so strangely, I felt that in actual fact the ominous sound of the wind we could hear only added to the feeling and atmosphere of the place, and the good thing was that it would show on the filming that we did.

Another challenge we had on this trip, was trying to entertain Rebecca's dear little Schnauzer. He was such a sweet dog, and of course working in a vet surgery myself, I couldn't help but love him instantly! He was clearly very loyal to Rebecca, and constantly wanted to be with her, so this is what posed another challenge for us while filming. While Patrick did the initial walk around with Rebecca Black; Jamie and I took it in turns to hold the little Schnauzer, by cuddling and making a fuss of him to keep him entertained. But, all the while he was keeping his eye on his Mum and trying his best to run around and follow her! He was definitely a character and even more lovable for it!

We then decided we would take a break, and Rebecca Black very kindly made some tea for us. The tea was made upstairs and then brought down the tower steps to where we were in the living area. I don't think any of us had really realised this, until all of a sudden we could just hear the chinking of cups. When we looked around, my heart jumped into my mouth. Rebecca was walking down the tower steps, at a fair speed, holding the tray which was crammed with cups, saucers, teapot and other things. She couldn't have been able to look at the ground at where she was going. I remembered from our filming earlier, that I had almost slipped myself on these stairs because of how narrow they were and uneven. One foot in the wrong place and you could easily lose your balance and go tumbling down, let alone when you're holding a heavy tray full of cups and other things.

Patrick and Karl stood up to go over and try and help her, by which time, she was already down the stairs and heading towards us with the tray. She looked quite amused when she saw our reactions. Indeed, I for one was amazed that she had not fallen or lost her balance, and thought she was incredibly brave to be descending those stairs at such a speed seemingly without even looking at where she was putting her feet. However, she lived here, and so I guess ascending and descending those treacherous stairs was now second nature to her – although all of us still admired her balance and ability to do this.

(Rebecca serving tea and telling us stories)

When the time came for us to do our investigation of the castle, it actually felt very daunting. Patrick had already picked up on quite a number of different spirits, and as we were walking around the castle we had come across a number of what I thought of as "secret doors" and passageways. Of course, some of these hidden away rooms and passages was where the psychic energy was actually the strongest, which then added to the slight nervousness we felt once we started our walk around with the voice recorder to see what we could get.

One of the most significant parts of the investigation for me was up in the tower room. There was what I can only describe as like a narrow hideaway or room, tucked away around one of the corners. The energy in this particular area felt very heavy and oppressive. We all felt uncomfortable sitting there, crammed into this small space and feeling the heaviness of the energy. Despite our nerves, we started to ask the Spirit questions as we normally did. The energy seemed to get stronger and stronger, until without warning, the voice recorder I was holding was knocked out of my hand. The sound of it falling to the floor was enough to make us all jump about a mile in the air. It didn't feel like a particularly nice spirit we were dealing with, and I didn't want to spend any more time here than I had to speaking with them. The others had the same opinion, so we finished asking our questions while picking up on the story of this man, before moving on to the next area.

The highlight for me on this trip to the beautiful Clonony Castle was when we went back outside the Castle at the end of our filming. To the side of the castle grounds there was a fenced off area with a strip of grassy field extending from the edge of the property. The field went down towards the castle and looked as though it even extended around to the back of the property. As we came out of the front door, we saw a horse that had wandered up the field and was standing placidly, watching us as if completely unaware of us being there. However, the wire fencing that kept him securely enclosed had been jostled from its place and was leaning precariously forward.

Rebecca shook her head and, clearly frustrated, set about righting the fence again. She wasn't fooled by the horse's charade of innocence, and from her reaction it seemed to me to be something that perhaps happened often! However, that wasn't what had caught my eye, as much as the beautiful four legged creature that stood in front of me. Being an animal lover and a person who also loves to horse ride, learning that Rebecca had a horse of her own was astounding. I was enthralled. Especially when she mentioned to us how, on occasions, she would saddle up and ride around the grounds at midnight. To me, it sounded nothing less than magical (if perhaps a bit cold during the winter). To round off this trip, we had a meal in one of the local restaurants 'The Old Fort', and we invited Rebecca to join us.

While we were eating, Rebecca told us that she was in school with Stephen Spielberg, that she knew George Lucas, and had worked with him on Raiders of the Lost Ark film with her late husband. Horses were part of Rebecca's life as her father had also owned a large stable in America. She told us that he had winners in some of the major races in the USA. One of Rebecca's great passions, one which I also share with her, is a love of writing! I learned how she was not only well established with her writing skills, but she was also an editor and tutor in the craft. Considering how much I have always loved reading and writing, I felt privileged to have met someone so skilled in this field. I didn't want the evening to end. It had been an amazing trip where we had met wonderful people. I had really enjoyed Rebecca's company and the filming at the castle had been exciting. Between us we had learned a lot about the history of the building, along with the haunted tales and stories of the ghosts and souls that were there. It was definitely a place I would never forget.

(Inside Clonony Castle)

The Bell

(Outside the "The Bell"- The "Jack The Ripper" graffiti wall art by Zabou)

Most of the filming we had done so far was in Castles and old houses, so we thought about other possible venues to conduct investigations. We came up with the idea of filming in a series of pubs. There are many pubs around that have amazing haunted tales attached to them that they were a good possibility to film in. Not to mention, the older and more ancient bars have a fascinating and often colourful histories that accompanies them. It stands to reason, that pubs are and always have been a focal point within towns, cities, or even communities. They are places where people of all different kinds of backgrounds come together, to chat and socialise, and it's often where the true characters of people can sometimes be seen. Pubs bring together people that have all kinds of stories that are individual and unique to that person. Friendships are formed, sometimes enemies are made, and the trials of life are often witnessed or at least gossiped about. For this reason, I find the histories of the different characters and communities surrounding a pub to be quite interesting and extremely vibrant and varied, in a vastly different way to castles and other more stately buildings. I thought it would be an interesting venture, and I couldn't wait to get started.

One of the first that we filmed in was a notorious pub near Whitechapel tucked away on a side street in the East End of London. When I say the pub is notorious, I mean notorious as a result of its history rather than because of the people that frequented there. It was the very same pub that is believed to have been used by Jack the Ripper himself – possibly as a means to identifying his potential victims during his grizzly crusade. It was called "The Bell".

When we arrived at The Bell on a glorious Saturday afternoon, the place was closed for us, as on the weekends its trade comes from the London business community who empty out of the city on the weekend. Entering the old building I sensed its atmosphere. I could almost feel echoes from the past seeping from the walls, hear the banter of the people that had been there in the past.... Yet, there was a distinct undercurrent of unease to the psychic atmosphere. It was like the feeling you have before a storm breaks, that transient feeling of impending danger. There was an electrical feeling in the air, one that causes you to be wary and stay alert. I didn't like this feeling. Part of me wanted to just leave it, let sleeping dogs lie and not explore it any further. Yet, part of me also felt incredibly curious, and I wanted to find out what actually did happen here and uncover the stories of the past that this building had hidden for so long. Jamie and Ben kept glancing at me, and I could tell by their reactions that they felt it too.

Patrick had already started picking things up the minute he arrived, as he normally does. He was picking up on things such as; the history of the building, the people who worked there, and some characters that had been here before along with their stories. He is able to pick up incredibly detailed information about everything, and it always amazes me. I observed that this ability of his seems to be one of the things that helps us form a mutual bond of trust and openness between both Ghostcircle and the people hosting us. They are also often impressed at the depth and detail of information Patrick is able to give them.

(Patrick interviewing Glyn in The Bell)

As for me, it took a while for me to be able to adjust fully to the strong atmosphere here. I knew I needed to let myself adjust to the atmosphere gradually. This is something that I had learned from our previous investigations. I started to become more sensitive, and so I deliberately kept my mind and senses closed down until it was getting close to the time when we would be filming. When you close down, it doesn't necessarily mean that you don't pick up or sense anything at all, that just isn't possible. Once you become sensitive to the Spiritual world, it is in a way like opening Pandora's Box. You will always be aware of it. When I "close down", I may still sense things such as the atmosphere of a room, or a general sense of a presence being close by in the room, but the information is much less detailed. You just don't pick up as much "closed down" as when you open up your senses to it fully.

Patrick started off with his usual walk around and I wondered what experiences we would have this evening during our investigation. Patrick seemed to be picking up a lot of activity and a myriad of different characters; although as yet we had not unveiled anything about the mysterious 'Jack the Ripper'. I had a feeling we would come across him a bit later. We started in the downstairs bar and it wasn't the only part that was haunted. The pub also had a second bar upstairs on the first floor which was mostly used as a function room. Above that was a stairs that led to a residential flat. Later on, when we were on the first floor, you could tell from just standing below that the flat above on the second floor was haunted too. It's strange, but you could just feel the palpable energy coming down from the floor above. For the purposes of our visit here though, we would only be investigating the ground floor bar and the function room on the first floor, we left the residential flat alone as the bar staff used that. We also planned to conduct a circle with the staff and some friends which we always enjoy doing, if time permits. We decided that the best place for this would be the basement area, as there was a strong energy here and it had enough space for us to conduct the circle comfortably without moving things around.

Once Patrick finished his walk around interview with Glyn the owner, it was time for Jamie, Ben and I to walk around and see what we could pick up from the Spirits there. I have to confess, this venue was perhaps one of the places I felt most nervous during all our time filming. We already knew that the infamous Jack the Ripper, who in life had been a serial killer, was said to have a connection with the pub as two of his victims frequented here during his life. One victim was recorded as being there on the night she was murdered. What if we came face to face with him? Jamie and Ben may have been safe, but all of his victims had been women, and so this made me feel even more nervous. I looked around at Patrick and Karl, who both seemed perfectly fine and unfazed. I reminded myself that nothing could hurt us unless we allowed it to, and I asked Spirit and my guides for protection. This brings me back to what I was saying previously in the book about fear. Fear, or the feeling of fear, is generated in your mind when you allow your imagination to take over your thoughts. It is important to remember that nothing can hurt you, unless you allow it to. Darkness can only come through by invitation. For example earthbound spirits or lost souls, who at first may appear to be quite intimidating mainly because they may have built up the energy to move things, thus causing poltergeist type activity. Most of these souls are not "evil", but are rather just confused, or frustrated, or sometimes simply trying to get somebody's attention. Quite often spirits just need to attract someone's attention, just so they can try to listen to their story and help them.

So as we started our investigation, I reminded myself of these things and started to feel a bit calmer. It was actually amazing the variety of different spirits that were there. Patrick had picked up earlier that there was a divide of classes here, as there were in most places during Jack the Ripper's time period. The ground floor bar was where the working class people would stay. They would only be allowed in this area, whereas the more affluent, upper class people in society would be allowed upstairs to where the function room now was. It was typical class segregation, and this showed even with the spirits we picked up on. In the ground floor bar we picked up on a couple of different characters there. Although it may sound predictable, and as it fits with the type of victim that Jack the Ripper used to target, we had picked up that this bar had been almost some kind of a haven for prostitutes. This was where they would pick up their 'business', and I got a very strong feeling that they used to look out for each other too. Patrick even picked up on the spirit of the 'madam' – the lady who used to oversee and look after her 'girls', who were the prostitutes working there. We ascertained, through our investigation, that these prostitutes seemed likely to be the only working class people permitted to go up to the second floor room, the flat area. They could do so, as long as they were accompanied/invited to do so by one of the wealthy patrons visiting there.

When we ventured up to the first floor to investigate the function room, this seemed me to be the main area of activity barring the basement. The energy was palpable as soon as you walked into the room. I kept being drawn to an area to our right hand side, and Patrick said earlier that he was picking up on a gentleman who in his lifetime used to sit at a table in the corner. He had dogs with him. He wasn't a man who you would want to cross, and according to the information we were picking up, he had less than ideal business dealings, although he was very well respected – perhaps through the fear that he incited. As I opened my senses further, I could pick up on this man's energy more clearly. He definitely had a commanding presence about him, and I sensed that even though on occasion he may not have actually said very much, everybody still took notice. He seemed to have a presence about him that was immediately noticeable when you entered the room – although I can't say I felt particularly comfortable with his energy.

I then turned my focus to the rest of the room, to see if I could sense any of the other spirits that were there.

It was a busy atmosphere, and I could sense that there had been a lot of people through here. Not particularly surprising, given that we were in a pub, but it was almost like feeling the ripples of a memory, a feeling induced by the threads of past events that had taken place and been absorbed by the building itself. Gradually, one of these threads became stronger and more intense than the others, and I became aware of the presence of another Spirit standing over by one of the other tables, on the other side of the room to where this other gentleman's presence was felt.

We had our meters on us – the voice recorder for EVP's and the K2 meter for detecting the energy of Spirits, and I concentrated on what I could pick up from the soul that was here. It felt like a distinctly feminine energy, so I knew we were in the presence of a female spirit. Her energy felt slightly timid, introverted, to me. She was a gentle soul, but I felt that she did want to communicate with us and tell us her story – hence why she was here with us now. We started as we usually do, by asking basic questions such as asking her name, and also her position here. We were trying to determine if she had been a visitor, a customer, or maybe instead a worker here. I believed that the latter was true. As we continued communicating with her, I could sense a slight undercurrent of fear from this spirit – as if there was a dark secret that she was almost afraid of voicing aloud. I looked at Jamie and Ben, and could tell they were thinking along the same lines. We were all wondering if this young lady had been one of Jack the Ripper's victims. I certainly suspected as such, but I didn't want to voice anything until we had more information – as I wanted to try and be sure that I wasn't reaching this conclusion due to my own pre-conceived ideas. Taking into consideration that we knew that Jack the Ripper most likely frequented here, and added to the fact that this pub was right in the middle of the area where the murders had taken place, I needed to make sure myself.

We asked if she was indeed a victim of Jack the Ripper, and if she had been murdered, to which she replied that she had. When we questioned her about her name again, we heard the response "Catherine Eddowes". Chills traced down my spine. If this was true, and we were actually communicating with the spirit of Catherine Eddowes, it was no wonder that she would be so troubled, having suffered a death such as hers and then to have that murder unsolved. It was made even more chilling as the place where Eddowes had been murdered, and where her body was found – Mitre Square, was only a five minute walk away from the pub in which we now stood. It was very possible that she could indeed have been working as a prostitute here in this building at that time, trying to make ends meet in the harsh slums of East End London, as so many young women like her were.

I could sense in her energy what I can only describe as a slight vulnerability. Now, whether that was originating from her, or simply from my own empathy with her plight, I don't know, but it made me feel protective towards her. I could still also sense the darker aspects that were here in this place, and I felt I wanted us to protect her from that as best as we could between us.

I felt a great sense of sadness at the lost opportunities Catherine and all the other ladies who had their life taken by Jack the Ripper. Each of them had potential in their lives, even if they had not been able to see it. Yes, they had been prostitutes, and they were working class people in their time; but I believe that they still had a chance at being able to overcome their hardships, yet the chance of reaching that potential had been taken from them. Some of the women, Catherine Eddowes included, also had children who themselves had to grow up without their mothers. Even aside from that, they still had a right to live just as much as anybody else.

We continued communicating with Catherine, trying if we could, to ascertain more information about her life and death, and her own account on what happened to her. A lot of the time, when we're investigating a place, I will pick up on things in the form of seeing pictures or visions – in other words, through clairvoyance. Occasionally, I will also hear certain phrases and pick up pieces of information clairaudiently, which has even at times been confirmed later when we have listened back to the EVP recordings on the voice recorder.

This time however, it was different. While I was seeing some images and clairvoyant information, the overwhelming majority of what I was gleaning was actually coming through what I could 'feel'. It was a new experience, and somehow made it all the more poignant when talking to the spirits that were here. I could connect with their stories on what appeared to be a much deeper level. The reason I mention this, is because there was a lot of information here just in the feeling of the atmosphere and the emotions coming from the spirits we were communicating with. I could feel the palpable comradeship between the women who had worked here.

They cared for each other deeply, as sisters would perhaps do, and had tried the best they could to look out for each other and cover each other's backs. It was clear they had been unsettled by the news that a serial killer who had a liking for prostitutes was prowling around the area where they lived and worked. They were trying their hardest to band together during uncertain times and all of this could be felt by me as threads of energy were weaving between one spirit and another; connecting them through the work that they did and the lifestyle they had shared. It was something quite unique that I had never experienced before, and it just highlighted to me how much we are all connected to each other, and also how the connections and relationships we share with people are remembered even after death.

Once we had finished investigating the first floor, we came back downstairs to meet up with Patrick and Glyn as Karl is normally only with us during our filming. We had a short respite before we were to begin the circle. Ben wandered off to do his own thing, while Jamie and I took in our surroundings. Out on the street, we could see a graffiti artist painting the side of the building, there were people bustling around going about their daily routines and rushing about. The sun was setting and hanging low in the sky, and just outside near the front of the pub, we could see a crowd gathering on the street in front of a young looking man holding a clipboard. They were soon going to be starting a "Jack the Ripper" tour – a famous attraction for any visitors to the area. I smiled at Jamie as we watched them. Little did they know that we were investigating and communicating with the real ghosts of that era! I wondered if the very fact of our presence here and what we had been doing throughout the day would heighten any activity that the participants of the tour would see. Without asking, it would be difficult to know, but anything is possible.

When we headed downstairs to the basement to prepare for the physical circle we would be doing, again you could feel the energy intensifying. I had to agree that it was the ideal place to hold the circle. As well as having enough space to accommodate all of the circle sitters, and the energy in order to hopefully allow spirit to give their evidence, it also had no windows! Now, I know that may sound like an incredibly strange statement, but in order to create the optimal conditions for physical phenomena to occur, it is usually best to have dim lighting – and even then to only really use a low red and blue light. Notice how I mentioned the use of *dim* lighting – it does not have to be completely pitch black. However, in order to create physical phenomena that people can see, Spirit use the energy we build in order to create photoplasm. Red and blue light, used in the right way, will not destroy this. However, white light, or any other light – coming through a window, for example – will destroy the photoplasm that is created, therefore making it much more difficult to create physical phenomena.

(In the basement of the Bell)

So, the fact that this room did not have any windows was like gold dust to us in this instance, as it made our jobs so much easier. Usually when we investigate a venue, if we hold a physical circle, we have to be careful that any "outside" light is minimised, which usually involves drawing curtains and blinds, and in a lot of cases also rummaging around for cloths to block any light sources that cannot be turned off, or to cover windows that do not have any curtains or blinds. We have had to do this so often that we carry, along with our other equipment; a selection of blacking cloths for this very reason! In light of this, finding the basement of "The Bell" pub in the east end was the ideal place for holding a circle, without masses of extra work 'blacking out' any windows.

As people started coming down into the room ready for us to begin our circle, I could tell some of them were slightly nervous. It's not surprising, and I think myself, Jamie and Ben all felt the same when we first participated in a circle. You don't know what to expect, or what is going to happen. Added to that, the knowledge of the history of the place, and the fact that it is connected with one of the most infamous serial killers in British history... even I was a bit nervous as to exactly what would happen. If there is one thing I've learnt, however, it's that we are always protected. Over years of experience of conducting these circles, Patrick had refined exactly how to provide protection for all of those participating in the circle, so that only well-intentioned spirits can come close and communicate with us. It is important to note, as well, that during a physical circle, at no point, ever, in all the times we have done our investigations, have I heard Patrick ask one particular spirit to come into the circle.

With his mediumship ability, if he can sense that a particular spirit is present, then, just as you may invite a friend to take part in something, he may ask that spirit if they can help build the energy, or stand in front of one of the circle sitters, so that we can feel and sense their energy and everyone in the circle can have a chance to witness the phenomena being produced. But I have never heard Patrick send out a general call, saying, for example "anyone that is here... come and talk to us!" especially not without first and foremost asking for protection from our guides and helpers. Personally, I always think this is an extremely dangerous thing to do. When you send out a vague invitation to the spirit world, it is like leaving your front door wide open, where anybody... whoever they are, good or bad, can come walking through. This is the same reason why Ouija boards are incredibly risky, because they encourage just this, and therefore is a magnet for more negative entities. It is an easy way to gain access into our physical world taking advantage of the enthusiasm of unsuspecting people. You could very well be speaking to a good sprit, but another bad spirit can come in and displace the good one, so you get unpredictable answers. When I first became interested in communicating with the spirit world, I too became enthused with the idea of using the Ouija board. It seemed the perfect and easiest solution. However, I found as soon as I started to consider using one, for the next week I just kept hearing stories on TV programmes of things that had gone horribly wrong when using them, people who had been seriously hurt, or reading about how dangerous they are, and hearing accounts from other people's experiences of entities that had tried to cause mayhem or harm through the use of these tools. I even saw some Ouija boards for sale in a shop, but something... some instinctive feeling just made me hesitate and stopped me from buying it. It very quickly turned me off of the idea of *ever* using one at all. Some of these may have been extreme examples I was hearing about, but looking back, I believe this was perhaps my own guide's way of giving a clear and timely warning against using such a thing. If a spirit wants to communicate with you, then they will come to you, and if mediumship is practiced in the right way, these are usually positive or benign spirits that mean you no harm. Remember – "evil", if you so term it, can only come through invitation, but by simply even using something like a Ouija board, you are giving out that open invitation – whether you know it or not.

Anyway, to continue with my account of our circle here: once everyone was seated in the circle, Patrick started in the usual way with an opening prayer of protection for everyone present. This is important usually for two main reasons. The first and most obvious reason is to give protection to everybody who is present. The second reason however, is that it also helps to bring everyone in the circle together and adds reassurance to people that actually, nothing bad will happen. Most of the time we recite the Lord's Prayer as the opening prayer, mainly because not only is it a well-known prayer that most are familiar with, but it also helps to affirm and reassure everyone – especially those who may be feeling nervous that we will be protected from anything harmful.

After we had completed the opening prayer, I could feel the energy in the circle settle, and knew that everyone was starting to relax into it and feel a little more comfortable. Patrick started to build the energy and then, as he usually does, called the circle sitters up one by one so that they could experience the phenomena. There was quite a big group of us on this occasion, more than I had expected there to be, but the circle seemed to be going very well none the less, and the energy was strong. There were a couple of people sitting to my left, and they leaned over and whispered, asking about what was happening. I could feel the energy was quite strong, so I held my hand out between us... I could see the blue rods of energy surrounding and extending from my hands. I did not say anything, but instead asked what they were able to see. They looked intently at my hand and the space surrounding it for a moment, before affirming they could indeed see the energy that was there. I then asked them to hold their hand out, and I kept mine where it was. Again, they could feel the energy between our hands quite clearly, although our hands were not touching. They were quite amazed, and I was pleased that they could witness this energy. For me, the greatest proof that anyone can have of what we know to be true... life after death, energy, the spiritual world... is to experience it for yourself, and it's always so gratifying when people are able to be open minded enough to experience this.

When it came to our pièce de résistance, the flower moving experiment, I was looking forward to seeing everyone's reactions. The people I had previously been helping sitting next to me, were given a flower. As Patrick explained the experiment to the group, he then asked everyone to watch their flowers to see if they were moving, I heard a couple of gasps beside me. The two people next to me had seen the petals of their flower moving. When they saw me, they commented on how amazing it was that the flowers were moving. I agreed. They then became really interested and asked lots of questions about the energy, and what was happening. By now, I had been to enough of these investigations and circles that I was able to answer their questions, but I was glad that they were curious and showing such interest in this and wanting to find out more. The more people can be open-minded to what they are experiencing, the more satisfying it is for us, as this is what it is all about – introducing more people to the spiritual world and showing them tangible phenomena, in order to show that life does continue after death and that there is more to this world than we can physically see.

England's Rose

(England's Rose, named after Diana Princess of Wales)

Another pub that we were fortunate enough to be able to film in was the lovely England's Rose, located in Oxfordshire. A lovely lady called Sheila owned and ran this pub, and she was generous enough to invite us there to investigate and see what we could pick up. Ben was absolutely thrilled as they also welcomed dogs, which meant he was able to bring along his beautiful dog Luna. She is an Irish terrier and the love of Ben's life!

We actually went to the pub twice. The first time was more for us to visit and get a feel for the place, and we also conducted a circle that night. Sadly, as pets are not allowed during the circle we do, this meant poor Luna had to wait outside of the circle room while we did this. The reason for this is to minimise any distractions or anything that might disturb the energy we are building up, and Luna is also a very energetic and playful dog and unlikely to sit quietly during a circle.

We could all feel there was a lot of energy here, and it was probably one of the places that I had felt so many different energies and Spirits. The landlady was telling us about all of the different phenomena they had experienced and everything that had been going on. I wasn't surprised. There was so much energy and so many different Spirits here that I would have been surprised had there not been any activity at all. However, saying that, I have to stress that I did not feel anything negative. There was also a separate building where there was another quite unpleasant spirit, which I will explain about in due course. But in the main pub building where we now were, I felt nothing malicious or negative. More like visiting Spirits and residual energies from previous times.

We set up the circle as usual, and I felt excited to start. The circle itself went ok, but I didn't feel it was quite as powerful as perhaps some of the others. Bearing in mind this was a pub, earlier in the evening a lot of the circle sitters had been drinking, and a couple were quite sceptical – both of which can affect the energy. It may have also been to do with the environment. We did get some phenomena, but it was more of an effort at times than other circles. That's not to say there was "less" spirit activity, or that some locations are "worse" than others. To say that is untrue. There are a number of different factors that can affect a circle – anything from technical issues, not enough red or blue light (the two lights which are used in circle), fear being experienced by anyone present can also be a major factor, therefore individual things can create difficulties when raising the energy at certain times, yet it doesn't make the circle any less successful. For the people with us in circle that night, they all experienced phenomena and had their own evidence of the paranormal, which I was pleased about.

I really enjoyed the evening, the harmony and people who attended enjoyed it, the atmosphere was very buoyant, and the pub itself was beautiful. I knew that looking back at the footage we would get a lot of phenomena coming through, and I was thrilled at the thought of Jamie, Ben and I starting our walk around.

On the night that we went back for our investigation, I wondered at what we would find, and we also realised that we would have the privilege of being able to also investigate the house that was to the side of the pub, where a lot of activity had again been reported. We made our preparations for the start of our investigation. I picked up our voice recorder and K2 meter, before heading to the back room where we had previously done the circle.

The back room itself was actually a very large old barn, but it was currently used for functions now and it had a small bar. The bar was at one end of the room, and then just in front of this, there was a bench with bar stools placed along it. There were more modern decorations that had been added to the room, including a few comfortable armchairs along the sidewalls of the room, and tables and chairs for when functions were being held. Along one of the side walls there was an old fireplace.

This is what drew our attention first, and so we headed over there and started our investigation. As soon as we reached the fireplace, we could all immediately sense the strong energy there. I remember I could smell smoke. It's always slightly difficult because when you are working with Spirit, as much as you must trust your intuition, you still need to be careful to keep a common sense view of things. For example, if you feel a draught but there is a window open right next to you, chances are that "draught" is actually coming from the window and has nothing to do with any ghosts. With time and experience, and as you connect to your own intuition more, you start to learn how to differentiate between the two, and distinguish what is being shown to you from Spirit, and what is actually being caused by something environmental.

I digressed a little there, as I mentioned a moment ago that I could smell smoke by the fireplace. Of course your first reaction and it was mine too; is to wonder whether you are 'actually smelling smoke' just because you are standing near a fireplace; or whether the smell of smoke is coming from a connection to the Spirit that was present. If one of the others confirms this, and there is no other reasonable explanation for this occurring, then it is safe to assume you are indeed picking this up from Spirit. I also try to keep an open mind until I have a little more information before making a judgement myself. In this case, Jamie and Ben said they could smell this too. The fireplace was closed and disused now. There was certainly no fire lit at the time, and no other possible source in the room that this smell could come from.

As I explored this connection further to try and get more information, I could see a gentleman in my mind's eye, and I heard the words "black trade". Jamie and Ben were also picking up information on this man, what he looked like in life and what his character was like. I remember we also picked up on the fact this gentleman liked to sit by this fireplace. His response to that was that it was good for getting rid of the evidence. We eventually realised by piecing the different snippets of information together, that in life he had attended the pub or Inn quite regularly, and most likely sat in this exact spot by the fireplace every night. He used to trade in illegal products – most likely with tobacco – hence the black trade that we picked up on. And of course, sitting by the fire meant that should anyone raise the alarm or try and catch them out, they had the perfect means by which to destroy any evidence.

After speaking to this man and relaying his story, we then moved on to where we thought we could sense more energy/spirit activity. When we conduct an investigation, and we move around a room, you may have heard me mention before the term 'following the energy'. What I mean by this, is that as psychic mediums, we can feel energy that is around us, and if a Spirit either crosses over or perhaps there's no more information left that we need to pick up, you can feel the connection fade. Equally, we are usually drawn to certain areas of a room – or indeed perhaps a different room altogether – if we sense the energy of a Spirit there. We generally follow our intuition. From my view point, the best way I can describe it is this; imagine there is a candle flame, and now imagine that you close your eyes, and reach out your hand towards the flame, so that it's near but not quite touching the flame. You would be able to feel the warmth and heat from the fire, even though you cannot see the candle or flame through your closed eyes. The big misconception we sometimes have is that if we cannot physically see something, then we assume that it cannot be real. What I would say to you is think about the wind. Even though you may see leaves blowing in the trees, you cannot physically see the wind itself. But you can feel it. It is a similar way that we pick up on energy. It is feeling something tangible even though you may not necessarily be able to see it. This the best way I can explain it, and is how we "follow the energy" when we conduct an investigation. We focus on where we can *feel* the energy, and go where our intuition guides us.

Returning to our investigation of England's Rose; after we had finished our communication with this man by the fireplace, we then felt a concentration of energy around the bar area at the top of the room. When we approached the front of the bar area, I realised I was picking up on a maid. Again, it may seem obvious to get this considering we were by a bar, but before I even mentioned it, Jamie and Ben again confirmed that they were sensing the same thing. I don't very often actually see spirits in the same way I can see living people. However, with this young maid, I could certainly see her, at least for a short while. I immediately felt compassion for her. She had a rough appearance, and seemed quite down trodden. I could see what appeared to be injuries of some kind on her body, as if she had been beaten. And I could feel the sadness coming from her. I could sense that the people whom she had worked for and with had not treated her very well in life. She seemed to have been neglected and ill-treated.

    I told the others what I was seeing, and we all agreed that we needed to help her. She needed release from her situation, and to realise that she was able to move on to where she belonged in the Spirit world, and that she could feel happy there. The three of us moved around behind the bar. I could still sense her standing with us, and I could sense that she was pleased for our help. We stood in a circle and joined hands – joining our energy together. I also said a prayer to ask for our guides and helpers to draw close to help us. I could sense them draw close to us, joining their energy to help us. We were going to do a spirit rescue to help this young lady. I said a prayer that she may be helped into the light, to go to where she belonged, and then focussed. It actually takes a surprising degree of concentration for something like this at times, because you are holding the connection in order to allow spirit guides and helpers to assist in "rescuing" the spirit that is trapped or feeling lost. Not that they would be helpless to do anything for the lost soul without us – for there are always those in spirit that are ready and able to offer help. With us being mediums, we are creating the connection and lending our energy to it, so it strengthens and aids the efforts of those in spirit trying to assist. As the saying goes – two heads are better than one!

As we stood there holding the connection, I could feel the energy getting lighter. The denseness and heaviness seemed to lift, and it was almost akin to the feeling you may have, when a weight is lifted from your shoulders. Instinctively, this is how I know our efforts are working and helping, because you can feel the change of energy. It is also interesting because sometimes you may find afterwards while going through the film footage, that you have caught some EVP's and spirit voices during the rescue. We later on heard a lady say, "thank you" on our microphone. Indeed, before now, we have had spirit voices captured on film thanking us for our help. It is always humbling to see how our efforts can really make a difference and help not just the other people we meet at the venues, but also our dear friends in spirit too. I felt glad that we had managed to help this lady, and hoped that she had now found the happiness that she deserved.

Once we had concluded our investigation in the main pub, we moved on to the house that stood a short way off to the side of the building. This was the part of the investigation I felt most anxious about. You could feel the energy even from outside. There was definitely an ominous feeling about this place, and I knew we would have to be prepared. Upstairs, there were a couple of rooms which were locked with combination locks, as they were used as separate accommodation rooms or offices for people, but we were starting our investigation on the ground floor.

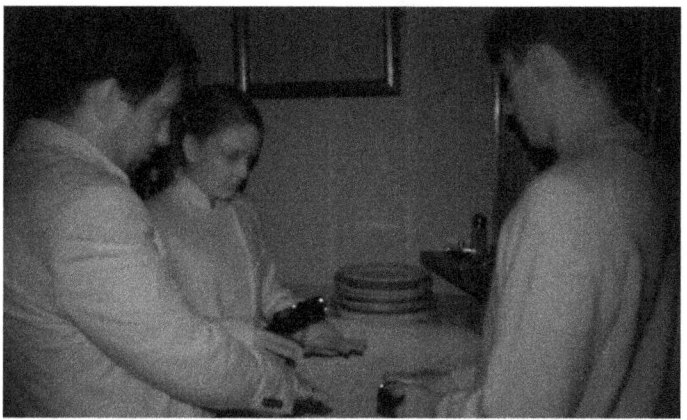

(Communicating with a spirit and releasing her in the old barn Restaurant)

As soon as we opened the door and stepped inside, the energy immediately intensified. I didn't like it, and I said so on the video. I could definitely sense there was something not very nice here. In my mind, I asked our guides to surround us with protection. It should not be assumed that we are not nervous during these investigations because sometimes we are; and although a spirit cannot hurt you unless you allow them to, your guides are always willing to step in and help if you ask them to. Additionally, it is always wise to remember never to become complacent. The moment you do is usually when you run into trouble. So, as I approached the house and entered the building I had asked for more protection.

The three of us stood in the entrance hallway looking around, trying to get our bearings, and to work out where we felt we needed to go first. We ended up going to the kitchen, which was just ahead of us on the ground floor. In actual fact, it was an open plan kitchen and lounge, and a considerably sized one at that. Each one of us was instantly drawn to the right hand side of the room. The energy here felt dense and oppressive, and I could feel it as a weight pressing in on me. I could also feel numerous spirits present already. There was a lot of unrest here and I felt instinctively that these spirits wanted their story heard. All except one! There was one spirit, a man, who we were all picking up on. He was the one who we felt was the cause of the unrest for the other spirits that resided here.

As we started to communicate more with this man, it became clear that he was not happy about our presence there. From his point of view, we were interfering and he didn't like it. We also had the sense of a lot of spirit children being here. There was certainly a lot going on. We spent some time on the ground floor trying to communicate with the man whose energy was the densest of all the others that we could sense. We wanted to try and get a better understanding of his story, including the incidents and activity that had been going on here. For myself, I could get a clear sense that he definitely did not want anyone here. There was hostility with him, not just towards us, but also toward anybody who entered here. As far he was concerned, this was *his* place, and he felt an intrusion into his space when people entered the house. Not to mention that he did not want anyone to discover what had gone on here. The dominant energy on this floor seemed to be of this man, who was very dense, and very heavy. After a while, it started to become almost overwhelming. We had now gained a better understanding of this man's character, and we still had the upstairs level to investigate too, so we decided to move on and try and communicate with some of the other spirits that were here before concluding our investigation.

Going upstairs I could feel the energy definitely felt lighter on the upper level, although there was still a distinct feeling of sadness in the air that could be sensed. We were first drawn to one of the bedrooms and when we entered it, again we could sense lots of children around us. I was sure at one point that I felt a child touch my hand, as if letting me know that they were there. Very unpleasant things had happened here. We could all sense the energy around us. There were the rods of photoplasm that we usually saw during these investigations when we held our hands in front of us. All of a sudden, Ben exclaimed he could feel vibrations through the floor, like footsteps, as if someone were walking up the stairs towards us. I had felt it too, and one look at Jamie told me he had experienced the same. Not only could we feel the footsteps, but we could hear them too. It was so incredibly real, that at first we felt sure that there must be someone coming up the stairs. Even though we knew this could not be true, that we were alone in this house, we had to check, but just as suspected, when we looked down the hallway and checked down the stairs, there was nobody there. The house was empty.

We also all agreed that we didn't want to leave this place without helping these spirits. We wanted to do a "spirit rescue" for them too. It was done similar to how we did it before with the maid in the main building. We stood around in a circle and held hands. Again, we called on our guides to help us, and I could feel the energy building around us as they stepped forward to help these children. All at once, I could see a golden archway in front of me. It was beautiful, bathed in light and actually seemed to be radiating light itself. As the guides stepped forward to help the children and spirits that were here, we could feel the energy becoming lighter, until it felt more peaceful once more, and I knew that those children had been helped.

It was such a wonderful feeling to know that we had helped them and to think that they were now at peace and not held here. We could feel footsteps again on the floor as Ben looked out the hallway from the room. His reaction showed he had clearly seen something. When we asked him, he told us he had seen someone at the end of the hallway, and then they had disappeared. It made all of us wary, because we knew that there was still a negative presence around. We felt that we had done what we could in this room now, and decided to move on to the next, which was the furthest room at the end of the upstairs hallway. The way the rooms in the house were set up, meant that each room had a pin code lock on them, as they were rented out for people to use.

As we reached this door, we keyed in the pin and tried to push it open. Nothing happened. We tried again, making sure we were putting in the correct pin, and still we could not get in. Then Ben tried, with the same result. Jamie was next to try, and even Karl, who was filming us, put the camera down to try and help with still the same result. The door just would not budge, no matter how much we checked the pin was correct or what we did. When we were just about to give up, we decided to try one last time. So, we put in the pin again and as I was expecting the same difficulty when I pushed against the door, amazingly this time it opened easily as soon as we had put in the pin. It was so easy it caused me to nearly fall through the doorway as I pushed the door open. We couldn't understand why we had so much difficulty in getting into this room, as we knew we had placed the correct pin (4 numbers) and all four of us in turn had tried to open it. We were convinced that the negative spirit that was here, or at least something, had been trying to prevent us from getting in.

The negative energy in this room rolled over us as soon as we walked in. This was definitely the domain of this man. I think all of us knew instinctively that the man we were sensing up here with us was the same person we had encountered downstairs. He definitely seemed to have the same air of menace about him. I could sense he was trying to intimidate us. To him, we were really encroaching on his patch and he didn't like it one bit. But I wasn't about to let him scare us. If you have a more negative spirit around, the one thing you must always remember is to never allow them to intimidate you. They cannot physically hurt you unless you allow them to, but they can feed off of your fear so it's important to stay confident in yourself and not allow yourself to give in to your fears. We didn't spend too long in this room, purely because we did not like the feeling in here at all. We could all sense that a lot of horrible things had happened, including domestic violence, and we didn't want to spend any longer in this room than was absolutely necessary.

Strange as it may seem, however, we were still all curious to find out more about this man's story. Even with spirits who are perceived as negative, they still have a story to tell, a past, just like everybody else, that shows all they have experienced and the life they had lead, and so, with the intention in mind to uncover more of the story of this place and the characters who had been here, we headed to the last room in our investigation.

The final room we investigated here was already unlocked, so thankfully, we didn't have a repeat of the problem we encountered entering the previous room. The energy in this room was markedly different from the others. Even now, it still amazes me how each room we go in or each separate area of a building can each have their own unique feel and atmosphere about them. It may only be a subtle difference, in some cases, but it's there nonetheless.

The energy I could sense in this room felt softer to me, more feminine, and not as harsh or aggressive as the other energy we had felt but still holding an undercurrent of sadness. There was still a muted, melancholy feel to the atmosphere in this room. Ben confirmed what I had picked up as he mentioned he could sense the presence of a lady here in this room. We all felt that she may be the mother of the children we had previously met and helped in the other room.

As we tried to strengthen the connection and communicate more with this lady, I suddenly felt a sharp pain in my wrists. It was incredibly real, and came on so suddenly that I knew this was connected with the lady. I wondered if she had perhaps committed suicide, but as I thought this, I could see her face in my mind's eye and saw her shaking her head at me. Then I heard her talk, and she told me that there had been a cover up. It was then I understood. She had been murdered, and whoever was responsible had cut her wrists to make it appear as if it was a suicide. I really felt sympathy for this lady, and relayed to the team the information I had just picked up.

We all agreed that we felt this is what had likely happened, considering the nature of the negative male presence we could sense. This lady, who had been his wife in life, was still here because she wanted her story to be told. She wanted the truth of what had happened to be exposed so that she could get closure. I could also sense that in life she had done everything she could to protect the children, and suffered greatly herself too.

As we concluded this investigation of ours, I hoped that the work we had done here and the spirit releases had helped not only those that were here in Spirit, but also the owner of the Rose pub and all the wonderful people that visited this place each day. It certainly held a lot of character, and a lot of history within its walls with many interesting stories to tell, although it had also, perhaps, been one of the most intense places we had investigated.

Our Sixth Sense

Now I have spoken about some of the different places we have been to, I would now like to explain a little more about the phenomena that we pick up, and answer some of the many questions I have been asked before about how I pick up and interpret the information that we are given from Spirit. When you say to people that you can see Spirits, you get a lot of mixed reactions. Some people think that you see ghastly horrible ghouls that jump out at you from the shadows, while those that are sceptical at worst think you're a loony tune who is a victim of your own hallucinations, and at best simply think you're weird. Other people may also sometimes think that you have always had this amazing ability and that you have always seen Spirits as clear as you can see living people. This, at least in part, is correct. Is it true that mediums are born with this ability? Yes! It is my belief that every single person is born with an ability to 'see ghosts' or communicate with the Spirit world – it's just that as we get older, social conditioning and the busy lives that we lead, cause us to lose touch with that inner voice of ours, namely our own intuition and "sixth sense". However, is it true that every medium sees Spirits clearly from the word go? Well, in my case at least, this was not true. It wasn't until my late teens that I started noticing that there was more to this world than what we can at first see. I remember one particular time early on when I was at work. I was on my own in the room, when I saw somebody open the door and walk in. I didn't see them clearly, just out of the corner of my eye, but thinking it was my colleague, I started talking to them. When there was no answer, I turned around only to find that I was alone in the room. I had been absolutely sure that somebody had been in the room with me. After asking around, I found that nobody had been to that particular room… I had been alone. However, one of my colleagues also proceeded to tell me that at times, other members of staff had reported seeing strange or unexplainable things, and for some, these experiences had led them to believe that maybe the place could indeed be haunted. Gradually as time went on, I started experiencing more and more of the paranormal and my psychic intuition grew stronger.

I found I could sense other people's emotions around me. At first I wasn't sure what it was and could not place where these feelings were coming from, but then something would happen, or a person would react in a certain way, and I would realise that I had been picking up what they were feeling.

It isn't always easy to deal with this ability, and you also need to learn how to shield or close yourself off from it. Otherwise it can quickly become overwhelming –

especially when you are picking up on things around you constantly.

I also started being able to sense the presence of my guide more. It is my belief that everybody has a Spirit guide who supports them during their life on earth. Not everybody senses them or even knows about them, but they are there none the less, constantly offering support and guidance to us through dreams, gut feelings, intuitive insights or 'coincidences' that occur.

Now, of course Spirit guides cannot live our lives for us, or make decisions for us – that is not their purpose. However, they will always be there to offer guidance and support to us when we are facing a difficult situation or choice, and always with complete unconditional love without judgement. What we then choose to do is up to us.

I also believe that Spirit guides 'tailor' the way they give their support to the individual person they are helping. As mentioned before they may use gut feelings, intuitive insights or perhaps put in place little 'coincidences' that seem to point in a particular direction. What works for one person may not work quite so well for somebody else, and so we will all experience their support and guidance in different ways, according to what works for us best. Most times they help without us even knowing it.

If you're observant enough, you may be able to notice certain patterns in the things that happen. For example, you may be thinking on how to solve a problem and find that the same topic keeps cropping up in conversations, or that you keep hearing the same phrases repeated by different people. You might even see things on posters, advertisements, or television; or notice persistent recurring thoughts or ideas coming into your head.

In my experience, this is usually Spirit's way of giving you a nudge in the right direction and sharing insights with you. Whether you then act on those insights is then down to you.

Methods of Communication

By now I hope I have given you a glimpse into my world. It's a world full of possibilities, a world without limits. On my travels with Ghostcircle one question that commonly gets asked not just to me, but to the rest of the team, is what is it like to be psychic? How do we get the information we pick up?

Exactly *how* a person intuitively picks up on pieces of information or Spirits that are around is as unique to each individual as fingerprints. Each person will experience the paranormal in a slightly different way, and so I can only give my own view and explain how I personally perceive the information and Spirits we come across.

Most of the time, if a Spirit or ghost is present; I mostly feel or sense their presence. It's almost like the feeling you get when you feel as though somebody is watching you, even though you can't see them. If I'm picking up on their appearance, I will either get an impression of what they look like, or I may see images in my mind of their features. Of course it stands to reason that during our investigations, if we are poked or prodded or pushed by a ghostly Spirit it is very much physical, exactly as it would feel if one of your friends poked or pushed you. The rest, although it may sound whimsical, is down to listening to your own intuition. You may be inclined to dismiss the information at first – I admit I have felt like doing that myself on numerous occasions – you dismiss it as being fanciful, or just your own imagination running away with you. But as more and more people confirm the facts you relate back to them, and it happens time and time again, eventually you begin to learn to trust what you are feeling, to listen to that inner voice, your gut feeling, that fills in the blanks of what you cannot physically see.

That is a brief explanation of how I perceive facts or information that a Spirit may want to relate to me. How they put it in terms of their physical appearance in life, or historical places as they used to be when the person was living their life here on earth. As a side note, my personal feeling and belief is that when a Spirit shows you a place where they used to live, or was prominent to them in their life, it is their way of projecting their memory of that place, to you. So you then try to perceive it as they saw it. Maybe, imagine that you have been abroad, or visited somewhere familiar. Now imagine that a friend asks you about the place you visited. Your friend hasn't been there before, has never seen it. How do you describe it to them? If there is no actual picture you can show them, how do you describe what it was like? You draw from your own memory and experience. I previously stated that thoughts are very much living things, and a memory is still a thought. You are still *thinking* about a place, a person or your experiences, and thoughts are energy. That is what I believe a Spirit is doing when they relay information to us. They are projecting their own memories and experiences of those places or events so that we can understand and build up a picture of what took place. It is a transfer of thoughts, a transfer of energy.

Another question I have been asked before, is how we can hear Spirits? And how can we talk to them? In some ways it is actually very similar to what I have just described, as it uses the same principle of transference of thoughts and energy. If you were to ask me how I actually hear them, I would say it depends. On certain occasions along with the rest of the Ghostcircle team, I literally hear the physical voice as if someone is talking in the room with us. Usually it may just be one word that is said, or a shout. If the Spirit is able to draw upon enough energy, we may even hear a full sentence. Indeed, there was one occasion where we were filming in a pub. We could hear all of this background commotion and noise and assumed it was people in the adjacent bar area talking only to discover later that there was no-one in the bar, and the voices were actually Spirits having a conversation.

The one thing that stands out about this, however, is that everybody in the room will hear the voice.

Everyone who is present will hear the exact same thing at the exact same time. Not only does this give us confirmation that nobody is making it up, but from a filming point of view it is one of the best and most exciting ways (along with the easiest way), we can document the evidence we come across.

Sometimes when a Spirit talks to you, you can hear their voice as either as sudden thoughts that enter your mind or as a separate voice entirely in the room. As your ability grows, you can have whole conversations with the Spirits who are communicating with you, and you know if it really is a ghost or Spirit giving you the information as you find it correlates to what is happening at the time, or else you find that once you mention what you have heard, somebody confirms that what you have said is true.

Epilogue

What I really enjoy most about filming with Ghostcircle is the fact that we are achieving something really worthwhile that will hopefully make a big difference in a lot of people's lives. Something that can give them comfort by letting them know that there is most definitely a life after physical death.

For me, the work that we do in Ghostcircle is not just about enjoying how much phenomena we can capture, or what we can as mediums pick up. Nor is it about scoring entertainment points by scaring people with ghostly stories of hauntings and portraying Spirits as being inherently 'bad' or 'evil'. In my experience this is not true – most of the time even Spirits who at first seem to be quite intimidating, or scary, may just be lost souls who are trapped here or cannot move on to the Spirit plane for a number of reasons. Their confusion, anger or frustration may therefore make them appear to be quite threatening (there are rare exceptions to this when we talk about other negative or evil entities, but it is not within the remit or purpose of this book to be able to go into that in detail).

No, the objective of the work we do is to educate and teach people, so that they might open their minds to the possibility that there is something more than what we can physically see. Once we realise this, it then brings comfort by knowing that our loved ones who have passed are ok, and are actually still living (albeit in a different way), and even watch over us until we can be reunited with them when it is our own time to cross over to the Spirit world.

I also believe that once people realise that our life here is not all that there is, that we then start to take more responsibility for our actions, because we hopefully start to realise the impact that our actions can have and the consequences that come from them.

I also love the fact that our work in Ghostcircle not only helps the people we come into contact with and meet, but also the Spirits we encounter too. There have been several occasions where we have 'rescued' Spirits who, for one reason or another, are stuck here on the earth plane. Sometimes it can be because they need help coming to terms with the fact that they have died, or it may be, particularly when something traumatic has taken place, that another Spirit is actually keeping them there. Other times still it can simply be because the Spirit in question wants their side of the story to be told, and wants the truth of a situation to be known – for example – when an injustice has occurred.

Whatever the reason, it is our privilege to be able to help them so that they may be at peace too. It is always humbling to know that we have made a difference to something or someone, and if we can also pass that knowledge on to help even yet more people... then all the better!

A lot of people may mistakenly think that being psychic and relaying messages from the dead is just a way of entertaining the masses, or perhaps just using tricks to impress. The real benefit of this incredible gift, however, is its ability to heal. Having the ability to see and communicate with the Spirit world allows you to connect on a much deeper level with people.

It is also important to relay the information you are getting with compassion and awareness of how that information will affect the people involved. Quite often, when somebody invites you in to help them, it is not only because they are curious about the Spirits that may be present there, but also that they are scared or unnerved at times by what has taken place, especially when you have very intense paranormal activity, such as poltergeist activity.

It is our job to take that fear away so that the people affected by it are no longer victims of the unknown but instead empowered by an understanding of what is going on so that they then have the tools to deal with it. That is also what the aim of this book has been; to educate, to inform and to shed some light on what actually goes on behind the scenes. It is said that the antidote to fear, is knowledge, and I also especially believe this to be true. If we open our minds, even just a little, to be receptive to learning a bit more about the Spirit world and how it *really* works, then we find our fear will dissipate. There is nothing scary or horrific about the Spirit world at all, and if we just take the time to explore what our friends in Spirit want to tell us and show us – that is when the true wonders of the Spirit world reveal themselves to us. So I hope this book has done just this for you. I also hope that it has given a little more information as to how certain paranormal phenomena appears to us; how we as a team in Ghostcircle work to capture it, and finally given you a little glimpse into the inside story!

www.ingramcontent.com/pod-product-compliance
Lightning Source LLC
Chambersburg PA
CBHW071453040426
42444CB00008B/1325